Elementary Harmony

PRENTICE-HALL INTERNATIONAL, INC., *London*
PRENTICE-HALL OF AUSTRALIA, PTY., LTD., *Sydney*
PRENTICE-HALL OF CANADA, LTD., *Toronto*
PRENTICE-HALL OF INDIA (PRIVATE) LTD., *New Delhi*
PRENTICE-HALL OF JAPAN, INC., *Tokyo*

THIRD EDITION

Elementary Harmony

WILLIAM J. MITCHELL

Professor of Music, Columbia University

PRENTICE-HALL, INC.

Englewood Cliffs, New Jersey

© 1939, 1948, 1965 by Prentice-Hall, Inc.
Englewood Cliffs, New Jersey

Library of Congress Catalog Card Number: 65-17800

Printed in the United States of America. C-25727

Current printing (last digit):
11 10 9 8 7 6 5 4

To My Mother and Father

whose assistance in bringing about this book reaches over many years

Preface

In preparing a third edition of *Elementary Harmony,* I have benefited by three factors: My own and my colleagues' experience in teaching from the book; a heartening general rise in the musical maturity and perceptiveness of music students; my own continued study of chromaticism. All have confirmed the value of the primary aims and methods of *Elementary Harmony.*

The aims in the present edition remain the same—the emphasizing of linear forces as the enlivening features of the essentially abstract nature of harmonic principles. The methods also remain the same—the stressing of differences between principal and dependent tones and chords, along with a refining of theories of root generation and inversion. Above all, aims and methods continue to have as their ultimate target the development of a student who exercises his own musical judgment, rather than one who memorizes sets of rules only to forget them.

Along with changes in detail, motivated by a desire for simplification and clarification, attention is directed to the following: In Chapter 2, the treatment of melodic structure has been much expanded; in Chapter 3, a more inclusive discussion of meter, tempo, and rhythm has been introduced; in Chapters 15 and 16, the discussions of sevenths and ninths have been more closely related to increasingly dissonant styles, and in the latter chapter more space has been given to an evaluation of so-called eleventh and thirteenth chords.

In revising and adding to exercises, a fresh emphasis has been placed on variety. Three and four part choral settings now appear in company with three and four part keyboard settings. The pedagogical goals of these and a description of each in terms of texture and notational practices appear in Chapter 9.

A teaching schedule was incorporated in the Preface to the second edition. Because of extensive revisions introduced into the third edition it has been replaced by a new schedule, still based, however, on a course that spends 28 hours a term for two terms on the book and its assignments. The time table is, of course, variable according to the talents and preparation of the students. As I have used the book, each chapter is assigned initially in complete form, but the meetings devoted to the chapter concentrate on major portions of it. Certain exercises, notably the Drills, can be worked out profitably in class at the blackboard or at the piano by either the instructor or a student accompanied by class comment.

FIRST TERM

CHAPTER	NUMBER OF MEETINGS	MAJOR SUBDIVISIONS
1	1	
2	2	1. *The Major Scale* *The Pure Minor Scale* *Mixed Scales* *Transposition of Scales* 2. *Melodic Analysis*
3	2	1. *Introduction* *Meter* 2. *Tempo* *Rhythm*
4	3	1. *Description* *Measurement—Absolute* 2. *Measurement—Relative* *Consonance and Dissonance* 3. *Melodic Attributes of Intervals* *Keys and Key Signatures*
5	1	
6	1	
7	3	1. Text of the Chapter 2., 3. Completion of Assignments
8	3	1. *Introduction* *Root Progression by Fifths*

It is my hope that the revisions incorporated into the third edition will lend their help toward achieving the only feasible general goal of the study of theory—the transformation of music students into musicians.

Completion of the third edition of *Elementary Harmony* has been greatly facilitated and expedited by the experienced counsel provided by my wife, Alice, who also read the manuscript and various proofs, and by the self sacrificing good behavior of my children, Susan, Aaron, and Philip.

WJM

Contents

Elementary Harmony

1

The Study
of
Harmony

The study of harmony embraces many concepts born out of musical practice. These range from the simple to the complex, from axiomatic relationships to highly involved derivatives. How can the exploration of so vast a body of procedures be ordered with the assurance that the beginning of the study will be in fact the beginning?

The first clue can be found in the single musical tone, for within its apparent isolation lies a universe of pitch relationships. Among these are the few that are needed to launch us into and guide us through the world of tones that constitute the materials of the study of harmony. The universe of pitch relations is the phenomenon of partial tones or the overtone series. Physically, the musical tone is comprised of a complex of pitches known as partials or overtones. Example 1 illustrates the first sixteen partials[1] of the heard or fundamental tone C. Bracketed tones will be explained in the section, *Unused pitches.*

[1] Or the first fifteen overtones. For purposes of calculation it is more convenient to reckon in partials, for their numerical order starts with the fundamental which is excluded from the overtones. However, both terms will be used in this study.

Ex. 1

Partials: 1 2 3 4   5 6 7 8 9 10 11 12 13 14 15 16 etc.

Fundamental tone

In this ultimately infinite series of pitch relationships the method of determining partials is quite simple: in order to locate the pitch of a partial, multiply its order number by the frequency of the fundamental tone. Thus, if C has a frequency of 64 cycles, middle C, the fourth partial will have 256 cycles (4×64). Further, the distance of each partial from the fundamental tone determines the degree of affinity between the two tones. This is confirmed by the fact that each partial, once it has appeared, reappears in every successive octave. Thus, C appears five times in the limited series of Example 1, and G, the third partial, appears three times, while E, the fifth partial, appears twice.

THE PARTIAL TONE SERIES AND MUSIC

These first products of the partial tone series are strongly suggestive of the prime materials of music. As indicated in Example 2, the fundamental and the second partial coincide with the octave of music; the fundamental and the third partial, reduced by an octave, coincide with the two tone relationship (interval) known as the perfect fifth; and the fundamental and fifth partial, again reduced, correspond with the interval known as a major third. Further, the series up to the sixth partial, often called the "Chord of Nature," reduces to a three tone chord or major triad. Each of these pitch relationships suggested by the strongest partials is of the first order of importance for the study of harmony. The octave of a tone is considered to be its transposition or duplication; the perfect fifth dominates and controls most musical relationships; the major third is a basic characterizing interval; and the triad is the model of all chords.

Ex. 2

octave   perfect   major   major
              fifth   third   triad

MUSIC AS AN ART

The relationship suggested by the physical nature of the tone to the prime materials of music is one of significant coincidence or analogy rather than fact. Its value for the study of harmony lies in the help that it provides in finding a point of departure. In fact, having gathered the first simple materials, we can now observe basic differences between the physical nature of the tone and the art of music.

Finite and infinite relationships

To start with, the generative principle of partials produces infinite results, but music thrives on a finite or closed system of pitch relations. In music, the twelve pitches that form our closed system are won by manipulating the prime intervals. Let us compare the physical generation of the partial tone, D, and the harmonic generation of the musical tone, D, both from the same C with a frequency of 64 cycles. Among the partials, D is ninth, hence its pitch can be determined directly as consisting of $9 \times 64 = 576$ cycles. In music the same D is reached harmonically by way of two perfect fifths, C to G, and G to D. Example 3 illustrates both procedures and includes an illustration of a way in which a chord on C can reach a chord on D, through a G chord, and how the D chord can return to the C chord by reversing the procedure.

Ex. 3

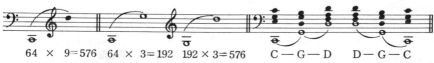

64 × 9=576   64 × 3=192   192 × 3=576   C — G — D   D — G — C

Simultaneous and successive relationships

Example 3 suggests another difference between the physical nature of the tone and the art of music. The principle of partial tones is realized instantaneously upon striking the fundamental tone. In music the analogue is the chord when its tones are struck simultaneously. But more basic to the nature of music are tones struck in succession, for the chord by itself is meaningless unless it is connected, through time, with other chords. It is the purposeful succession of tones and chords that gives music its form as an art. Thus D, as the ninth partial, is implicit in every fundamental C, but in music the relationship between the tones C and D is established most fruitfully in stages temporally realized.

Derived pitches

Music also employs pitch relations that are not readily discernible in the partials series. Models for the perfect fourth (C to F), the minor third (C to E–flat), and the minor triad (C- E–flat—G) can be found by mathematical calculation or by a musical manipulation of the first won materials, but not as direct relationships between a fundamental tone and its partials, as can be seen by re-examining Example 1. Yet these are also among the prime materials of music.

Unused pitches

Further, not all partials have counterparts in music. The bracketed B–flat, more correctly minus B–flat of Example 1, is not identical with the B–flat of our tonal system. In fact, it is precisely at this point that the physics of the tone and the art of music depart from each other. The seventh partial from C (64 cycles) has a frequency of 448 cycles, but the B–flats of music, measured from the same C are, depending on the tuning system, 456.1 (equal temperament) and 455.1 or 460.8 (both products of the systems known as just intonation). The pitch difference between the seventh partial and equal tempered B–flat is roughly one-third of a semitone. As in the case of the determination of D, the B–flat of music is won by indirect means, by the musical manipulation of the prime materials. When the higher partials of a tone are explored, many more pitches foreign to the major-minor tonal system make their appearance. Note that in the fourth octave of Example 1, three foreign, bracketed tones occur. These and all others hold a positive interest for the study of acoustics, tone color, and for experimental purposes as in microtonal music, but for the student of harmony in search of a starting point, they offer no help. The truth is that even the first won materials, the perfect fifth and the major third, undergo slight modifications of pitch in order to create, through equal temperament, the finite system of twelve pitches that constitute our world of tones.

CONCLUSION

The simple relationships set forth in Example 2 are all that are needed to begin an ordered study of harmony. From time to time they shall be called upon to clarify musical procedures. But in the end it will be found that techniques of music will be best learned by making the musician rather than the laboratory technician our guide.

2

Scales—Melodic Analysis

Description

The major ($+$) and minor ($-$) scales, which form the basis of this study of harmony, are diatonic: that is, they consist melodically of a succession of whole and half steps. The major scale has two half steps: one between the third and fourth degrees and the other between the seventh and eighth degrees. The remaining adjacent degrees are separated by whole steps. Numerals as well as names are used to identify the degrees or steps of the scale. Numerical designations, which follow the ascending melodic order of the scale steps, take the ordinal form: that is, we speak of the "first step," "the second step," etc. The origin and significance of the names applied to each degree is obscure, being based on various practices at various times. For

Ex. 4

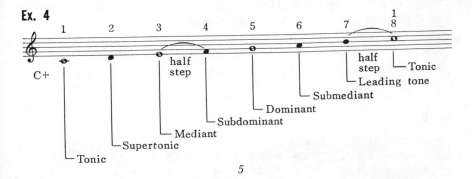

example, subdominant means melodically, "below the dominant," just as supertonic means "above the tonic." But harmonically, subdominant refers to the tone, in this case F, that has a position just as far below the tonic as the dominant is above. Hence it means "lower" or "under dominant." The wisest procedure is to memorize the degree names and to apply them without regard to supposed origins.

Principal tones

The scale represented in Example 4 represents in summary form the first melodic attributes of music. Each of the degrees has characteristics which contribute to our feeling of orientation, our "sense of key." The tonic degree stands at the beginning and end of all activity; it is the tone to which all others are related and ultimately toward which they move. Hence it is the most stable. Through its powers of attraction we are able to locate and characterize the other degrees. Thus while the tone F has many meanings, when it appears as a member of the scale of C major it becomes solely a fourth step, bearing a fixed relationship to the tonic degree. In addition to the tonic, two other degrees, the third and the fifth, standing in the relation of partials of C as in Example 5, partake of the tonic qualities of stability and attraction. These three degrees, called principal tones (P.), form points of repose in the scale.

Ex. 5

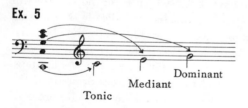

Tonic   Mediant   Dominant

Dependent tones

1. As passing tones. The remaining degrees of the scale are active and dependent in nature. Their original melodic function is to act in the capacity of passing tones (p.), tones struck in stepwise transition from one principal tone to another. Between the fifth and eighth degrees there are two passing tones; between the other degrees only one.

Ex. 6

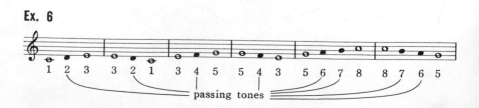

1 2 3   3 2 1   3 4 5   5 4 3   5 6 7 8   8 7 6 5

passing tones

2. *As neighboring tones.* Dependent tones also serve the function of decorating the principal tones. A decorating or neighboring tone is always adjacent to the tone it decorates. It exists in two general forms, complete (n.) and incomplete (i.n.): complete when the motion is from a principal tone to its neighbor and back to the same principal tone; incomplete when the motion is either from a principal tone to its neighbor followed by a leap, or a leap to a neighbor followed by its principal tone. Both are illustrated in Examples 7*a* and *b*. The double neighbor in various forms appears in Example 7*c*.

Ex. 7

3. Passing and neighboring tones combined. Example 7d illustrates ways in which passing and neighboring tones appear in direct succession. In such cases, the passing tone or neighbor is simply delayed in its entrance or in the completion of its motion. Hence, these are extensions rather than violations of our definitions. On occasion, neighboring tones are to be understood as substitutes for the passing tone, as in Example 7e, where the neighbors trace a circuitous route from one principal tone to the other. Between the fifth and eighth degrees one of the two passing tones is sometimes omitted to create a unique extension of the passing relation as in Example 7f. Although the elision creates the appearance of a neighboring tone, the difference lies in the fact that the neighbor characteristically changes its direction (compare Example 7f with Examples 7a, b, and c) while the passing tone does not.

4. Incidental leaps. When principal tones are struck in direct succession, one or more of them often plays a supporting or subsidiary role as indicated in Example 7g. Such tones are called incidental leaps (i.l.) and are frequently played in company with passing and neighboring tones as in Example 7h. Note that the incidental leap is differentiated from the passing tone and neighbor in that it is characteristically approached and quitted by a leap.

Melodically active half step relationships

The leading tone has a marked tendency to progress to the tonic because only a half step separates the two degrees. This salient melodic relationship is of great importance in that it directs attention to the tonic degree and serves to point it out as the center of orientation. The half step relationship also makes the fourth degree active in the direction of the third, a principal tone. When these two progressions are combined they establish the position of the tonic of the scale with a conviction that cannot be duplicated in the original diatonic form of any other scale or mode.

Ex. 8

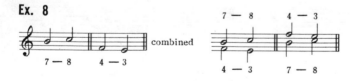

THE PURE MINOR SCALE

Description

The pure minor scale contrasts with the major. It partakes only by analogy of the relationships that are characteristic of the major scale. This can be seen in the fact that one of the principal tones, the third degree, is not a partial tone of the tonic. It acts as a principal tone only because it is in a position similar to that of the third degree of the major scale.

Ex. 9

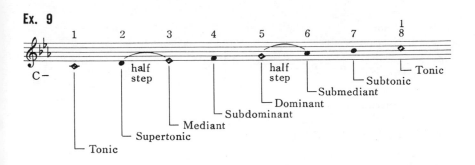

The leading tone

The minor scale imitates the major scale distinction between principal tones—the first, third, and fifth degrees—and dependent tones—the second, fourth, sixth, and seventh degrees. However, because the seventh (here called the subtonic) and fourth degrees are a whole step away from the eighth and third, there is no strong key-defining drive in the pure minor. To correct this serious deficiency the seventh step of the major scale is borrowed on those occasions when it is necessary to point out the position of the tonic degree. This is done by raising the subtonic degree of the minor mode, thus making it a leading tone.

Ex. 10

MIXED SCALES

1. Minor

The use of the major-scale leading tone in the minor results in a mixed scale, inasmuch as it is partly minor and partly major. This practice of transferring a tone of one mode to the other may be extended to the sixth step. Three mixed minor scales may thus be created.

Ex. 11

Pure Minor

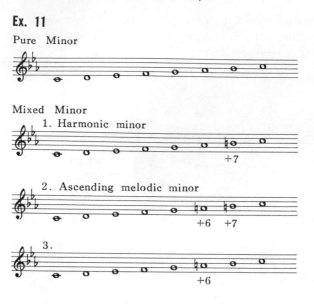

2. *Major*

The process of mixing degrees works in the opposite direction also. Degrees of the minor scale are frequently substituted for original degrees of the major scale. Mixtures are possible only between modes that have identical tonic degrees: C major and C minor can interchange elements but C major and D minor or C major and A minor, for example, cannot.

Ex. 12

Pure Major

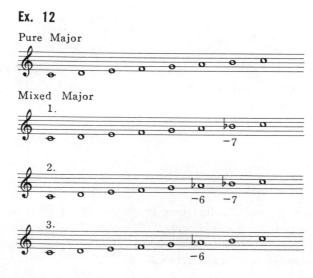

Examples of mixtures

Mixtures are variants of original tones and have been used by all composers. The most common mixture in minor comes from the substitution of the major-scale seventh step as a corrective for the original seventh step of the minor. Examples can be found on practically every page of music written in the minor mode. The opening bars of Mozart's A-minor Sonata, K310, are characteristic of the use of the leading tone.

Ex. 13

The first theme of the slow movement of Brahms's Fourth Symphony is a striking example of the substitution of C-natural and D-natural, the sixth and seventh steps of E minor, for C-sharp and D-sharp, the sixth and seventh steps of E major.

Ex. 14

TRANSPOSITION OF SCALES

To construct a major scale from any tone other than C, or a minor scale from any degree other than A, accidentals must be used to preserve the correct order of half and whole steps.

Ex. 15

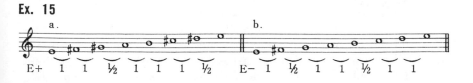

In constructing scales in which many accidentals are used, it is important to remember that within an octave each degree appears once and once only.

Ex. 16

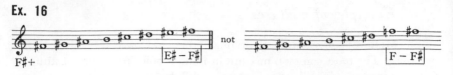

These accidentals, which establish the correct sequence of steps of the major and pure minor scales, are assembled in orderly groups called key signatures and placed at the beginning of compositions and wherever long-lived changes of key take place. Tables of key signatures appear in Examples 80 and 81. The accidentals that introduce mixtures or other transient alterations are placed directly before the note affected.

Ex. 17

MELODIC ANALYSIS

Detailed analysis

The scale as it exists in the abstract form of Example 4 reveals specific features of organization which can be stated profitably in a more generalized form: Melodic construction is characterized by various kinds of motion between points of repose. Thus stated, dependent tones are the active, onward moving or decorative elements of melody; principal tones are the initiating and terminating points. It is the nature of melody to exploit segments of the scale, to expand first on one tone and then on another in the course of its unfolding. As this happens, surrounding tones take on dependent meanings in accordance with the ways in which they serve the temporary dominating or principal tones. Hence, *any* degree of the scale may act as a dependent or principal tone, according to the contours of a melody.

Let us examine the details of Example 18. Brackets point out the limits of each melodic unit or group. Bars 1–2 present a melodic situation that is quite clear; F is a passing tone between the principal tones E and G. In bars 3–4 a different but analogous situation exists; G now plays the role that F played in bars 1–2. Hence, it too is a passing tone moving within the limits of F and A, established by the shape of the melody. Similar distinctions exist in the remaining bars: F passes between G and E in bar 5; E passes similarly between the principal tones D and F in bar 6, and D passes between E and C in bars 7–8.

Ex. 18

Broad analysis

Melodic analysis must not stop at this point, for the melodic groups of Example 18, each with its own principal and dependent tones, succeed each other in a manner that makes a broader, comprehensive sense. Note how the activity of bars 1–2 gives emphasis to G, how bars 3–4 subserve A, and how bars 5, 6, 7, 8 emphasize G, F, E, D, C respectively. This broader analysis reveals a more abstract level of construction with its own principal and dependent tones, as illustrated in Example 19*a*. Example 19*b* represents a way of combining both levels of analysis, that related to detail and that related to inclusive structure. Tones of broad structural meaning are notated as half notes, while the sense of the details is indicated by means of slurs.

Ex. 19

Observe that certain tones which are considered principal tones in the detailed analysis become dependent tones in the analysis of broader structure. Thus in Example 18, A (bars 3–4) and F (bar 6) appear as principal tones, since they play this role in the smaller world of melodic detail. But in the inclusive analysis of Example 19*a* they become a neighbor and a passing tone respectively. This is not a contradiction, for each tone is to be evaluated in the terms set by the guiding context, small or large. Note also that the broader analysis tends to follow the stepwise pattern of the scale, as in Example 4.

Additional examples

The variety to be found in melodies is virtually endless, and the challenge to the analyst often becomes severely taxing. Eventually he must be equipped with a knowledge of harmonic progression, voice leading, design, and rhythm, among other things, in order to cope with the problems that arise. Even though such equipment lies ahead of us, certain recurrent features of melodic activity are within our grasp.

In Example 20, rhythmic manipulation offers a challenge which can be resolved through broader analysis. In this case, three reductions are required in order to represent schematically a striking and imaginatively disguised rhythmic and motific parallelism which relates bars 1–2 to bars 3–4. Example 20*a* presents a passing motion in A minor from E to C; 20*b* indicates the extensions of the tones E (bars 1–2) and D (bars 3–4) through the introduction of upper neighbors; 20*c* is a detailed analysis, the smaller contexts being indicated by slurs. C–sharp and D–sharp are a chromatic neighbor and a passing tone. Observe in 20*d* how Chopin's rhythms artfully disguise the melodic parallelism that is revealed by his phrasing slurs.

Ex. 20 [1]

The busy incidental leaps of example 21*a* submit readily to the magnetic organizing powers of the stepwise progressions of 21*c*. An intermediate reduction appears in 21*b*. Many instrumental melodies are built on this kind of dominating step progression in the midst of rapid arpeggiation or passage work. Such constructions depend as much on the persuasiveness of stepwise motion as on the logic of chord progressions.

[1] Chopin, Mazurka, Op. 7, No. 2, beginning.

Ex. 21[2]

Example 22 illustrates melodic structure as an agent of musical design. Bars 1–4 introduce a two tone stepwise relationship, C-sharp to B, which reaches its ultimate goal in the A of bar 8. But before the goal is reached these two tones are repeated, thus contributing features of broad melodic structure to a miniature two part design. In this case, the analysis of detail is simple. However, in order to clarify the relation of broad analysis to design, two illustrations, Examples 22*b* and *c* have been introduced. The slurs of 22*b* point out various balancing motific relationships, while 22*c* indicates by way of two beams the common melodic goal, A, of the repeated C-sharp to B motion.

Ex. 22[3]

CONCLUSION

Examples 20, 21, and 22 have been introduced in order to present various aspects of melodic structure in company with: 1. rhythmic manipula-

---

2 Bach, *Well tempered Clavier*, Bk. II, Beginning of Fuga XV.
3 Mozart, *Don Giovanni*, "La ci darem."

tions (Example 20) ; 2. concurrent leaps and steps (Example 21) ; 3. features of design (Example 22). All of these factors are vital parts of our study and will be called upon frequently in the chapters to come.

For the rest, the student of harmony must be adept at both detailed and broad analysis, for one will help him resolve questions related to the immediate choice of chords, while the other will guide him in regulating the general flow of the harmonic current.

3

Meter, Tempo, Rhythm

Music is a temporal art, and is thereby differentiated from the space arts, such as painting and sculpture. Three interrelated factors are directly concerned with time in music. They are: 1. Meter, or that which measures; 2. Tempo, or that which determines the speed of measurement; 3. Rhythm, or that which is measured. All of these, separately and in combination, are exhaustive subjects which might easily fill the remaining pages of this book. The aim of the present chapter is to establish certain ground rules which will serve the limited purposes of the student embarking on the study of harmony.

Suffice it to say that if the subject of music and time were pursued farther, it would embrace additional systematic factors and many others that defy orderly classification. Some of the latter would be based solely on conventions. In the 17th century, for example, the metric signature was, in many cases, an indication of pace or tempo just as much as it was a kind of measurement. In the 20th century, on the other hand, meter often plays the role of rhythm, and rhythm becomes a form of meter.

But even within the limits of definable conventions, there are marked differences of procedure, based on the musical personalities of various composers. Thus, Beethoven's choice of meters is not the same as Mendelssohn's or Brahms's, for each exhibited marked individual characteristics in this respect as well as in others. The performer who would play a work in triple meter by Beethoven must know as much about the composer's individual metric preferences as he knows about the abstract nature of meter, tempo, and rhythm.

The immediate purpose of our study is to establish the basic and generally applicable distinctions which may help to eliminate gross misconceptions, lead to modest refinements, and clear the way for deeper understanding.

METER

The musical metric system stands in relation to the passage of time as a ruler stands in relation to space. The ruler divides space into convenient regular units. Meter does the same with time. Details of the metric system are pulses or beats, fractions of these, combinations of pulses to form bars, and the grouping of bars to form phrases. Beyond this the system of meter includes groups of phrases to form sections and the grouping of sections to from compositions. Each measurable composition is provided with its system of measurement through the metric signature and the regularly recurring bars and bar lines.

The metric signature

The metric signature, two numerals placed at the beginning of a composition and at those subsequent points where the meter changes, discloses in its upper numeral the kind of meter that will scan the piece, and in its lower numeral the kind of note that will receive one beat. For example, the metric signature $\frac{2}{4}$ indicates a simple duple meter with one beat to each quarter note.

Ex. 23

The numerals that form the metric signature are expressed in cardinal form: we speak of "two-four" meter, not "two-fourths," for the metric signature is not to be considered a fraction.

Kinds of meter

1. Simple. Meters in their simplest form are either duple, consisting of one strong and one weak pulse to a bar, or triple, consisting of one strong and two weak pulses to a bar.

Ex. 24

a. Simple duple meter

b. Simple triple meter

2. *Compound.* The duple and triple units of simple meters may be combined or compounded to form longer meters of four or more pulses. Example 25 illustrates three instances: quadruple or four beat (25*a*), nonuple or nine beat (25*b*), and septuple or seven beat (25*c*). In example 25*c*, Brahms's metric signature indicates that the meter is made up out of successions of triple and duple pulses. An alternate method is to represent in the metric signature the total of beats in each complete bar (in this case, seven) and to employ a dotted bar line to show the inner groupings of pulses, as in example 25*d*.

Ex. 25[1]

----

[1] Ex. 25*b*, Beethoven, Sonata, Op. 79, 2nd movement.

Ex. 25*c*, Brahms, Trio, Op. 101, 2nd movement. Later, in the same movement, Brahms combines ⅜ and ⅝ as a form of ⁵⁄₄ with triplet subdivisions.

The distinguishing feature of compound meters is the presence of differentiated strong pulses. The bar line points out the position of the stronger pulse. In all, we find three levels of pulsation: the heavier strong pulse, the lighter strong pulse, and the weak pulses. But, as we have seen, there are only two levels of pulsation in simple meters: the heavy pulse and the light pulse.

The difference becomes apparent when the effect of each is compared with the other, as in Example 26. In two bars of quadruple meter (C or $\frac{4}{4}$) there are two equally strong pulses, one at the beginning of each bar, two less strong pulses, and the weaker pulses. But in four bars of duple meter ($\frac{2}{4}$), covering the equivalent span of time, there are four equally strong pulses and four weak pulses.

Ex. 26

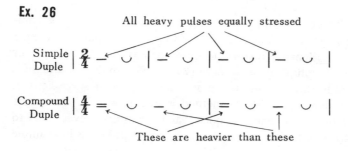

The more usual compound meters are $\frac{4}{4}$ or C, $\frac{6}{8}$ (sometimes $\frac{6}{4}$), and less frequently, $\frac{12}{8}$. In the twentieth century there has been a marked increase in the use of "irregular" compound meters, consisting of such as seven, ten and eleven beats.

Divided beats

Each metric beat may be broken up into fractional beats. The normal divisor that organizes this smaller world of beats is two; one beat becomes two half beats, one half beat becomes two quarter beats, one quarter beat becomes two eighth beats, and so on. Thus if the time signature indicates a quarter note as the unit of pulsation, each quarter note beat may divide into two eighth notes, each of the eighth notes into two sixteenth notes, and so on. In divided beats, the first note of each group is more accented than the second, just as the first whole beat of a bar is heavier than those that follow within the bar.

Ex. 27

The less usual divisor in the metric system is three. A whole note may be divided into three half notes, a half into three quarters, and so on. When a triple grouping of note values is intended, it is indicated by the numeral 3 written over or under the tones.

Ex. 28

Haydn

etc.

The same practice extends to all unusual divisions of lengths, as suggested by Example 29 where subdivisions into groups of six and seven notes predominate in a meter in which four sixteenth and eight thirty-second notes are the normal divisions.

Ex. 29 [2]

etc.

Combined beats

Similarly, pulses may be combined to form composite pulses. Again, the principle of organization is duple. When the unit of pulsation is a quarter note, two pulses may combine to form a half note and two half notes may combine to form a whole note.

Ex. 30

The metric system of note values that follows from this duple arrangement of pulses is shown in Example 31.

---

2 Brahms, *51 Exercises for the Pianoforte*. No opus number.

Ex. 31

Notes

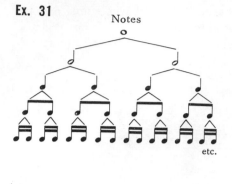

etc.

Equivalent Rests

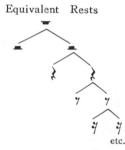

etc.

Dots

The dot extends the length of the note after which it is placed by one-half of its value. Whether the inclusive length is to be performed as a triplet or one and one-half duplets depends on the meter. A dot placed after a quarter note in ⅜ meter forms a triplet; but in ²⁄₄ meter it forms one duplet and a half, as illustrated in Example 32. Within the bar, the dot forms a duplet and a half or a triplet according to the normal grouping, duple or triple, of the subdivision.

Ex. 32

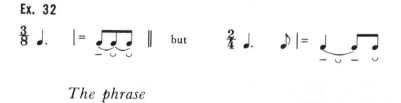

The phrase

Just as beats combine to form bars, so do bars combine to form phrases. Here too the organizing principle is duple. The usual phrases are two, four, or eight bars long, and they generally include two equal hemiphrases.

Ex. 33

Beethoven Op. 28 Trio of scherzo

A triple organization is less frequent. The folk tune "Die neue Jagd" consists of three six-bar phrases, each one of which is made up of two three-bar hemiphrases.

Ex. 34

Die neue Jagd

TEMPO

The "normal" pace and the quarter note

The basic unit of pulsation in our metric system is represented most frequently by the quarter note. Quarter notes succeeding each other at a walking pace represent a kind of ideal or normal speed, from which all other note values take their measurement. However, there are several kinds of walking paces, from sauntering to purposeful to hasty. There is a similar kind of variability in the "normal" pace of the quarter note. Whether it shall be sauntering, purposeful, or hasty depends on tempo indications, metronomic markings, and the character of the music. The usual tempo markings from slow to fast are the Italian terms; largo, adagio, lento, andante, moderato, allegro, vivace, and presto.

When indications of pace suggest rapidity, as allegro, vivace, or presto, the speed of the quarter note shifts to the fast area of its normal speed; when the indications are slow, as in largo, adagio, or lento, the quarter note shifts to the slow area of normality. Sometimes, as in the case of $\frac{2}{2}$ or alla breve (¢), the quarter note pace becomes so fast that the half note assumes the role of pacer; conversely, when the tempo is very slow, the eighth note assumes this role, as in the case of the slow $\frac{6}{8}$.

Tempo and notation

The variability of the speed of the quarter note from one tempo to another accounts for an apparently strange notational practice. Slow movements, marked adagio for example, frequently contain notes of smaller value, such as 32nd, 64th, and even 128th notes. But fast movements often employ nothing faster than 16th notes, and in fact seem to be characteristically notated in eighth, quarter, and half notes. The reason becomes clear when it is realized that in slow tempos the quarter note pace is relatively slow, hence the smaller note values are required for the expression of quicker subdivisions. On the other hand, when the quarter note pace is fast, the usual quick values can be expressed by sixteenth and eighth notes. Instructive examples of this practice can be found in Beethoven's Sonate Pathétique, opus 13. Compare the different note values within the first movement as the tempo changes from Grave to Allegro. Also compare the notation of the second movement, Adagio, with that of the third, Allegro.

Tempo and compound meters

It was observed earlier that the distinguishing feature of compound meters is the presence within the bar of three levels of pulsation; the heavy strong pulse, the lighter strong pulse, and the weak pulses. Tempo bears an intimate relationship to further classification of compound meters. Let us take the case of $\frac{6}{8}$. Should it be regarded as a form of duple meter, consisting of two pulses each subdivided into triplets, or as a form of triple meter, consisting of six pulses organized into successive groups of three pulses each? It can be either, depending on the tempo. A fast $\frac{6}{8}$ sounds like a kind of $\frac{2}{4}$ with each beat subdivided into triplets. A slow $\frac{6}{8}$, with its 8th notes emphasized, sounds like two bars of $\frac{3}{8}$ with differentiated strong pulses. The difference is illustrated in Example 35.

Thus tempo bears a critical relationship to our concept of meters. It can transform the nature of $\frac{6}{8}$ and other meters as well. Beethoven's scherzos are

Ex. 35[3]

a. Presto con fuoco

b. Largo e mesto

so rapidly paced that conductors beat only once to each bar of $\frac{3}{4}$. In such cases, the listener tends to group two or more bars into his own "compounds" by regarding two, three, or four bars as special types of $\frac{8}{6}$, $\frac{9}{8}$, or $\frac{12}{8}$. But as usual, Beethoven's metric signature is correct, for only by using the short bars and quarter notes of $\frac{3}{4}$ could he portray the dynamic power of his scherzos.

RHYTHM

Note lengths and accents

A consideration of the precise way in which the lengths and accents of tones may suggest and express a meter brings us into the province of rhythm. Of the many combinations of these two rhythmic elements that are

[3] Ex. 35a, Beethoven Sonata, Op. 31, No. 3, 4th movement, bars 64–70.
Ex. 35b, Beethoven, Sonata, Op. 10, No. 3, 2nd movement, beginning.

possible, our immediate concern is with those which, in the simplest or clearest way, establish and validate one or another meter. We naturally accord rhythmic weight to relatively long notes and assume that they start on a stronger pulse than that on which they end. The first metric constructions that we would assume in the rhythmic groups in Example 26a are those in 36b.

Ex. 36

Hence the simplest rhythmic confirmation of a meter occurs when:
1. Held notes extend from a strong metric pulse to a weaker pulse.
2. Longer notes are assigned to the beginning of the bar.

Rhythmic groups

Rhythmic figures or patterns of notes in music form into groups which together make up phrases. The beginning of a group may start on the first metric pulse, in which case the bar line serves as a dividing line separating one group from another, as in Example 37a. The groups, however, may also start with an anacrusis (a weak beat or the weak part of a divided beat). When such is the case, the bar line should be thought of as a point bridged by the group, as in Examples 37b and c) rather than as a mark of separation.

Ex. 37

RELATIONSHIP BETWEEN METER AND RHYTHM

Meter is defined by fixed standards of measurement; rhythm deals with varying lengths and accents. The question arises: how is it possible to tell that a certain meter correctly measures a composition and another does not? All rhythms that can be measured by meters have in them a principle of regularity. The lengths and accents of the notes vary not chaotically but with reference to the principle of regularity which is recorded by the metric system. The fluid play of rhythmic lengths and accents represents manipulation of the metric system of regular beats and lengths. Thus, a composition in $\frac{3}{4}$ meter lives in a world where the normal length is a quarter note and the normal rule of accent is one heavy beat followed by two light ones. In this world, rhythmic elements lead preferably not a strict conformist's life, but one that accepts and interprets generously the spirit of the law.

The first principles of rhythmic-metric agreement, as discussed above, will prove most helpful if they are employed as a general guide and starting point for rhythmic measurement. There are in fact many ways in which rhythms may be metrically scanned. Thus, although Example 36 part 2 suggests a triple scheme of measurement, the scheme is capable of two metric placements, one with the bar line placed after the first note as indicated, the other with the bar line before. Both are possible, of course, but each expresses a different accentual nuance, as indicated in Example 38.

Ex. 38 [4]

Often, musical rhythms are influenced by the patterns and gestures of the dance, the rhythms of speech and poetry, or by the desire of a composer to depart from a simple measurement in order to create greater rhythmic interest. Above all, the rhythms created by chord changes, often called harmonic rhythm, are vital factors in the determination or affirmation of meters, as we shall have opportunity to observe in the following chapters.

---

[4] Ex. 38a, Beethoven, First Symphony, Menuetto, beginning.
  Ex. 38b, Brahms, Second Symphony, 3rd movement.

Melodic measurement

A working knowledge of the interrelation of meter and rhythm can be gained by writing in the bar lines of simple measurable melodies and deciding upon their meter. This task approaches that of every composer, who must notate his works rhythmically and metrically in such a manner that the performer will know exactly how to play them. In one sense our problem is more difficult, for we shall start with a melody whose accentual personality is presumably unknown to us; but in another sense it is easier, since the essential note lengths shall have been fixed.

Look first for rhythmic groups and their repetitions. It is safe to assume in simple cases that the barring of a group will fit its repetitions as well. Note that the melody of Example 39 contains only two different groups, one (*a*) repeated twice, and the other (*b*) repeated once. The first adds up to six quarter notes, but *b*, more helpful to us, consists of only three. Melodically and rhythmically *b* suggests $\frac{3}{4}$. $\frac{6}{8}$ is possible, too, but *a* refuses to be measured naturally by it.

Ex. 39

In placing the bar lines, make use of the principle that longer notes gravitate toward the head of the bar. Play your setting with exaggerated emphasis on the heavy pulses and strict adherence to the value of each note. This test will expose any divergence between your conception of the rhythm and your notation of it. The correct setting appears in Example 40.

Ex. 40

For our needs as students of harmony, exercises such as these will suffice. Actually the relationships of meter, tempo, and rhythm often grow very complex. The composer must decide whether his composition notated in, let us say, sixteenth and eighth notes in a given tempo and meter will assure him of a performance which is an accurate projection of his conception, or whether it would be better to write it in eighth and quarter notes with appropriate modifications of tempo and meter. A study of Beethoven's sketch books will reveal the difficulties faced by him when he notated many of his works.

4

Intervals

Description

An interval is formed by two tones struck simultaneously or successively.

Ex. 41

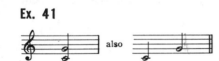

Intervals are known by the exact distance from one of the tones to the other. These distances, however, are more than mere measurements; they represent critical meanings to the musician. For example, the distance from middle C up to E is known as a major third, and the distance from middle C to F-sharp is known as an augmented fourth. But the difference between the two intervals is more than a difference in size; it stands for a difference in effect, significance, and the way in which each is put to musical use. In this sense, an interval is a relationship[1] between two tones. In the sections that follow, our first concern will be with interval measurement, that is, with the interval as a *distance* between two tones. Later, starting with the section, *Measurement—Relative,* we shall turn to the interval as a *relationship* formed by two tones.

---

[1] There is another way of expressing the interval as a relationship: The two tones form a ratio derived from the partials series (see Ex. 1). Thus, C : E = 4 : 5 = major third. Similarly, C : F-sharp = 32 : 45 = augmented fourth.

Numerical size

The complete name of an <u>interval embraces two terms</u>, one standing for its <u>numerical size</u> and the other for <u>its quality</u>. The numerical size is the number of degrees on the staff from the lower tone to the upper tone:

Ex. 42

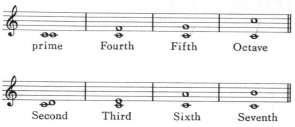

In measuring an interval that is greater than a ninth, an octave may be subtracted from its numerical size. Tenths, elevenths, twelfths and so on are usually called thirds, fourths, fifths, and so on, unless specific sizes are being discussed.

Ex. 43

The smallest interval, for practical purposes, is the half step or semitone, of which there two kinds: the diatonic half step (or diatonic semitone) and the chromatic half step (or chromatic semitone). As illustrated in Example 44*a*, the diatonic half step is a form of second, while the chromatic half step (Example 44*b*) is a form of prime or unison.

A given pitch may be notated in more than one way, as indicated in Example 44*c*. Such variants in notation are said to stand in an *enharmonic relationship*. Thus, an enharmonic notation for D is C–double sharp; another is E–double flat.

Ex. 44

Quality

The qualitative term distinguishes chromatic differences among intervals of the same numerical size. In Example 45 all of the intervals are seconds, but in quality they are dissimilar.

Ex. 45

The qualities that are of concern to us are:

- + major
- − minor
- p. perfect
- d. diminished
- a. augmented

To facilitate the determination of the qualities of intervals, place primes, fourths, fifths, and octaves in one group, and seconds, thirds, sixths, and sevenths in a second group:

Ex. 46

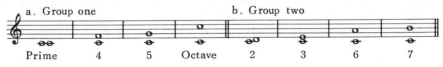

1a. When the upper tone falls in the major scale of the lower tone, the interval is *perfect* if it belongs in the *first* group:[2]

Ex. 47

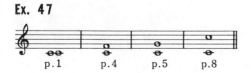

---

[2] The intervals in Ex. 47 to 53 are limited to those that relate directly to our applied work.

1*b*. When the upper tone falls in the major scale of the lower tone, the interval is *major* if it belongs in the *second* group:

Ex. 48

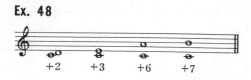

2*a*. If the interval is a chromatic half step smaller than perfect (first group), its quality is *diminished*:

Ex. 49

2*b*. If it is a chromatic half step smaller than major second group), its quality is *minor*:

Ex. 50

3. If it is a chromatic half step smaller than minor (second group), the quality is *diminished*:

Ex. 51

4. If it is a chromatic half step greater than either perfect (first group) or major (second group), its quality is *augmented*:

Ex. 52

The intervals that are of primary importance in this study of harmony are, in summary:

Ex. 53

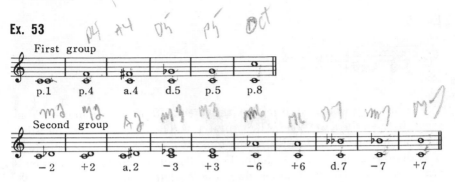

First group

p.1   p.4   a.4   d.5   p.5   p.8

Second group

−2   +2   a.2   −3   +3   −6   +6   d.7   −7   +7

Inversion of intervals

An interval is inverted when, by an octave transposition of either tone, the original upper tone becomes the lower tone. The sum of an interval and its inversion is nine:

Interval	1	2	3	4	5	6	7	8
Inversion	8	7	6	5	4	3	2	1
Sum	9	9	9	9	9	9	9	9

One quality, perfect, remains unchanged by inversion; all other qualities change to their opposites:

+ becomes —
—   ”   +
a   ”   d
d   ”   a

Ex. 54

p.5   p.4   p.5   p.4   +3   −6   −3   +6   d.5   a.4   a.2   d.7

Application

The system that has been employed in the preceding paragraphs for the determination of qualities is only of limited value. To apply it one must think of each interval as if it lived in a private world, dissociated from any context. Let us suppose that, for example, in a composition in C minor the system should be applied to the interval B–natural—A–flat:

Ex. 55

The first step would be to remove the interval from its C minor environment. Because the lower tone is B–natural, this tone for purposes of measurement would have to be considered the tonic of a major scale. The only form of A that lies in B major is A–sharp. The A–flat of the interval in question is two chromatic half steps lower than the A–sharp which forms a major seventh with B; hence the interval turns out to be a diminished seventh.

Ex. 56

MEASUREMENT—RELATIVE

Introduction

The absolute system of interval measurement is useful only until the ability to recognize intervals immediately develops. Of permanent value, however, is a knowledge of the positions occupied by intervals in major, minor, and mixed scales. To return to Example 55 for a moment, it is of lasting value to know that the interval formed by the leading tone and the pure minor sixth step (B–natural to A–flat in this instance) is always a diminished seventh, for this fact is directly related to musical meaning and use. When an interval is identified through its context, it is measured relatively. It is no longer thought of as self-dependent but as part of a series of relationships which bring order to music.

Interval positions in the major scale

Let us consider the intervals formed by the steps of the major scale. Note in Example 57 that the minor second and its inversion, the major seventh, appear twice, being formed by steps 3–4 and 7–1. The major second and minor seventh appear five times in the positions indicated. There are similar multiple appearances for all other intervals, except for the diminished fifth and its inversion, the augmented fourth. These are formed only by the fourth and seventh steps.

Ex. 57

Key defining intervals—major mode

The single appearance of the diminished fifth and the augmented fourth, its partner by inversion, isolates the pair from all other intervals. Further, the position occupied by the pair, embracing the fourth and seventh steps, is such that a normal melodic motion of the tones drives to the eighth and third degrees, thereby pointing out clearly the location of the tonic degree, as indicated in Example 58. When all factors are considered—the unique sound, the position in the major scale, the melodic tendency toward the tonic and third degrees—it can be readily understood why the diminished fifth and augmented fourth can define a key center so convincingly. Example 58 illustrates this "key defining progression."[3]

Ex. 58

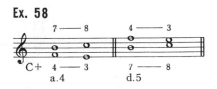

---

[3] Review, *Melodically active half steps*, Ch. 2.

Interval positions in the pure minor scale

A table similar to that of Example 57 can be constructed for the minor mode. Note in Example 59 that, although there are the same number of appearances for each interval and its inversion as in Example 57, the placement varies. For example, the minor second and its inversion, the major seventh, appear twice, but now they are formed by scale steps 2–3 and 5–6 rather than 3–4 and 7–1. Note also that the diminished fifth-augmented fourth pair occupy the second and sixth steps of the pure minor scale.

Ex. 59

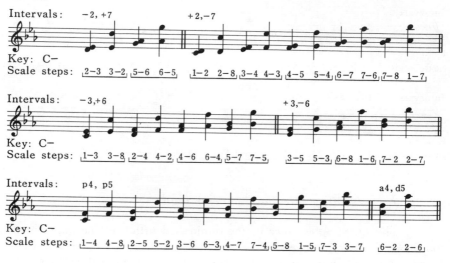

Intervals: −2, +7   +2, −7

Key: C−
Scale steps: 2–3 3–2, 5–6 6–5, 1–2 2–8, 3–4 4–3, 4–5 5–4, 6–7 7–6, 7–8 1–7,

Intervals: −3, +6   +3, −6

Key: C−
Scale steps: 1–3 3–8, 2–4 4–2, 4–6 6–4, 5–7 7–5, 3–5 5–3, 6–8 1–6, 7–2 2–7,

Intervals: p4, p5   a4, d5

Key: C−
Scale steps: 1–4 4–8, 2–5 5–2, 3–6 6–3, 4–7 7–4, 5–8 1–5, 7–3 3–7,   6–2 2–6,

Key defining intervals—minor mode

For key defining purposes, the unique pair (dim. fifth, aug. fourth) is not as well placed as in the major mode, for the normal melodic motion of its tones leads to the third and fifth degrees rather than to the eighth and third. As a result, the complete progression tends to move away from rather than toward the tonic degree. In Example 60, E-flat major is more readily heard than C minor.

Ex. 60

d.5   a.4

C− 6 — 5   2 — 3
    2 — 3   6 — 5

Eb+ 4 — 3   7 — 8
     7 — 8   4 — 3

?

This ambiguity is corrected by raising the seventh step of the minor mode, thereby creating an imitation of the key defining progression of the major mode, as illustrated in Example 61.

Ex. 61

The introduction of the corrective leading tone creates a mixed minor scale, out of which comes another unique pair, the diminished seventh and augmented second, representing the leading tone and the pure minor sixth step. This pair also has key defining capacities, as indicated in Example 62. Because they represent a contrived relationship, the mixing of major and minor scales, they are a step advanced in complexity beyond the diminished fifth and augmented fourth. These latter are native to the major mode and are simply transplanted to the minor.

Ex. 62

Other placements of the diminished fifth and augmented fourth can be found in mixed scales. These lead away from the tonic degree and therefore have no key defining value, as in Example 63.

Ex. 63

Modulatory intervals—major and minor scales

As shown in Examples 57 and 59, most intervals appear more than once in major and minor scales. If the single appearance of the diminished fifth in the major scale limits its meaning to steps 7–4, the multiple appearance of other intervals suggests that each can have as many meanings as it has step positions. For example, the major third, C to E, represents steps 1–3 in C major. But major thirds appear three times, totally, in the major scale— on 1–3, 4–6, and 5–7. C–E, as a major third, may represent any of these, not only 1–3 in C major, but also 4–6 in G major, and 5–7 in F major, as indicated in example 64a. How can each of these meanings be clarified? A rudimentary means, the key defining progression, is already available. As shown in example 64b, the affiliation of C–E with each of the three keys can be established by placing after it the key defining progression proper to each key.

Ex. 64

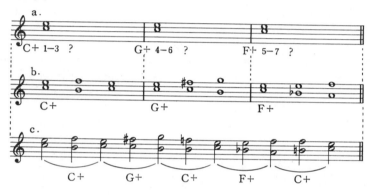

Intervals with multiple positions, then, make it possible to move or *modulate* from one key to another, as shown in Example 64c.

In order to assign a particular step meaning to a major third (again C–E) in the minor mode, the key defining progression must be borrowed from the tonic or parallel major mode. Thus, C–E may stand for 3–5 in A minor, 7–2 in D minor, and 6–8 in E minor. It will be established in each of its step meanings by use of the key defining intervals, 4–7–sharp of the keys of A, D, and E respectively, as shown in example 65b.

Ex. 65

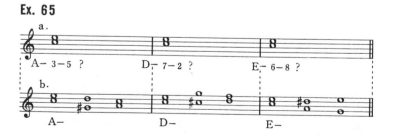

Summary

The major scale contains a unique interval in a unique position, with pronounced melodic tendencies. This interval, the diminished fifth (or augmented fourth) can be employed to define, stabilize, or isolate a key. It serves the same purpose when transplanted to the minor mode.

All other intervals appear more than once. They have as many key affiliations as the steps that they represent. These intervals may be employed to move or modulate from one key to another.

Hence, in the miniature world of intervals, two basic techniques of music are discernible: key definition and modulation. Key definition depends on unique meanings, modulation on multiple meanings.

CONSONANCE AND DISSONANCE

A limited number of intervals are called consonances; the remainder, dissonances. The distinction is a product of musical usage, but a basis for it can be found in the abbreviated partials or overtone series, as discussed in Chapter I.[4] Consonances are those intervals that reside in one form or another in this series; dissonances do not.

Primary consonances

The strongest consonances are those that duplicate the relationship of a fundamental tone to one of its overtones, as illustrated by Example 66.

Ex. 66

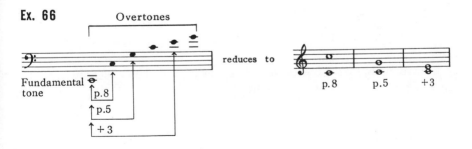

---

4 See Ex. 2.

To these three primary consonances the unison consisting of nothing more than the duplication of a single tone may be added.

Ex. 67

p.1

Secondary consonances

Secondary consonances are those intervals whose tones are related through the fact that both refer to a common fundamental tone.

Ex. 68

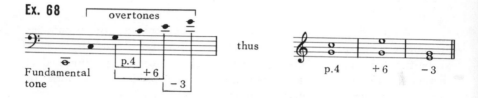

Another way in which certain of these weaker consonances are won is by inversion.

Ex. 69

p.4   − 6   + 6

The result is four more consonances which, added to the four primary consonances, give as a total of eight:

Ex. 70

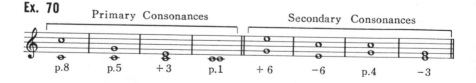

The distinction between primary and secondary consonances

Primary consonances are those intervals whose tones stand in the relationship of a fundamental tone to one of its overtones; secondary consonances are those intervals whose tones stand in the relationship of two overtones which have a common fundamental tone. The difference in the origin of the two kinds of intervals accounts for their difference in effect. Primary consonances are stable and self-subsistent. They depend on no additional factor to prove their stability. The consonance of the other group is unequivocally possible only when the original fundamental tone is actually or contextually present. Hence, the perfect fourth, probably the most evasive of intervals, will prove to be perfectly stable when the parent fundamental tone adds its confirmation to the real relationship of the tones involved. The same is true of major and minor sixths.

Ex. 71

All consonant in the
presence of the Fundamental tone

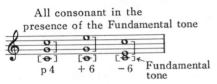

When this witness to the consonance of the perfect fourth and the two sixths is missing, a conflict arises. Our ears tend to give the lower of the two tones the importance of a fundamental tone. As a fundamental tone, however, it can enter into consonant relationship, as we have already seen, only with tones a perfect octave, fifth, or major third above it. Our ears, having established the character of the lower tone, now regard the upper tone as an obstacle in the way of the realization of one of these fundamental-tone-overtone intervals. For this reason, the perfect fourth will tend in such situations to move to the nearest primary consonance, the major third and the sixths will tend to move to perfect fifths:

Ex. 72

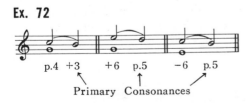

The minor third, however, does not submit so readily. The only primary consonance near it is the major third. A movement to the latter interval involves a chromatic change:

Ex. 73

-3 $+3$

Such a change is much more complex than our diatonic ears will ordinarily deem necessary. Confirmation of the stability of the minor third comes from its inclusion in the major triad, the most consonant of all chords. It arises as a by-product of the association of two primary consonances, the major third and the perfect fifth, as indicated in Example 74.

Ex. 74

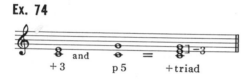

$+3$ and   p 5   =   +triad

Yet, a token of the greater consonance of the major third can be found in the long standing practice of ending minor mode compositions with a major triad containing the "Picardy" (that is, major) third as in the C minor Prelude of the Well tempered Clavier, Book I.

The only constant consonances then are the primary consonances. The secondary consonances, with the exception of the minor third, are stable in the company of the original fundamental tone; otherwise they tend to move to the nearest primary consonance.

Dissonances

All other intervals are dissonances. The tonal relationships which they represent are not to be found in the abridged overtone series. As a result of this fact, dissonant intervals create a tension which is most simply released when one or both of the tones move to the nearest consonance, primary or secondary.

Ex. 75

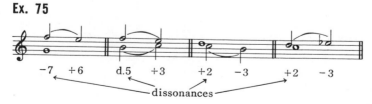

-7 $+6$ d.5 $+3$ $+2$ -3 $+2$ -3

dissonances

The distinction between consonance and dissonance is a product of musical usage, but it is supported by analysis of the overtone series. Certainly, the basis of the distinction rests less with "good sounds" (consonance) and "bad sounds" (dissonance) than it does with qualities of stability and tension, based on the difference between closely and remotely related sounds. Primes, octaves, perfect fifths, major thirds, and minor thirds too, are stable. Major and minor sixths, and perfect fourths can be, and often are, less stable. But seconds, sevenths, augmented fourths, and diminished fifths are tense, active sounds that most readily discharge their energy by moving or resolving to consonances. Such a condition does not rule out the use of consecutive dissonances either as a refinement or extension of techniques of resolution, or as an independent technique to be employed in an appropriate style of composition. The terms consonance and dissonance are arbitrary, but the difference between stability and tension is not. Although it would be easy to abolish the terms, it is not so easy to abolish the tonal attributes that they stand for. For our purposes it will be most helpful to accept the terms as well as the qualities represented by them.

MELODIC ATTRIBUTES OF INTERVALS

Consonance and principal tones

The distinction between the stability of consonant intervals and the tension of dissonant intervals is closely allied to the melodic character of the tones involved. In Example 76 the tone E when given consonant support might very easily stand for a melodic principal tone, the beginning or end of a motion, but when made into a dissonance its melodic character changes to that of a dependent tone decorating the bracketed D.

Ex. 76

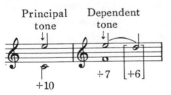

This fact establishes two pairs of relationships between the horizontal and the vertical: principal tones and consonances are one pair; dependent tones and dissonances are the other. The three-toned succession E-D-C in Example 77 stands for two principal tones, E and C, connected by D, a passing tone. To add vertical conviction to this melodic analysis the principal tones demand consonant support, which is provided by the stationary middle C. The dependent tone forms a major ninth with this accompanying tone, a dissonance whose vertical restlessness is a companion to the melodic activeness of the passing tone.

Ex. 77

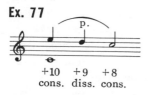

An opposite arrangement of consonant support for the dependent tone of Example 77 and dissonant support for the principal tones of the same example produces results completely at variance with our original melodic analysis. The dissonant E in Example 78 can now be heard only as a decorating tone to the D, which assumes a new meaning, while the C presses on to the bracketed B. The melodic results of this setting are that D and B become temporary principal tones and E and C become dependent tones.

Ex. 78

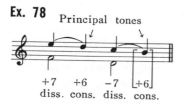

Consonant support of dependent tones

Thus principal tones, to be heard as such, demand consonant support. Dependent tones, although dissonant by origin, may be given consonant support without impairment for their original nature, which is determined by melodic context. In other words, a passing tone or neighboring tone will continue to function as such whether it is left in its original dissonant form or whether it is given the reinforcing support of a consonant interval.

Ex. 79

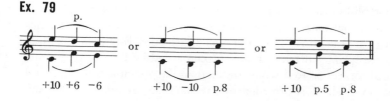

It is this fact, that original dissonances may be transformed into consonances, that enables us to win new supporting tones or intervals and eventually, new chords. To summarize this relationship between melodic function and intervals:

1. Principal tones demand consonant support.

2. Dependent tones, although active by nature, may be given consonant support without impairment of their original melodic function.

KEYS AND KEY SIGNATURES

The systematic arrangement of keys and their signatures is based on the close relationship of tones that stand a perfect fifth apart. Starting from the key of C major, which has no accidentals, the key whose tonic degree is a fifth above is G major, which has one sharp in its signature. Continuing upward by perfect fifths from G major, the next key is D major, then A major with three sharps, and so on until F sharp major is reached, where a halt may be called.[5] Starting from C and moving downward by perfect fifths, F major with one flat is reached; then B flat major with two flats, and so on to G flat major with six flats, where again a halt may be called.[6] The two ends of this motion by fifths, F-sharp in one direction and G flat in the other, stand in enharmonic relationship to each other. Hence they form a link in what may be regarded as a cycle of keys.

Ex. 80

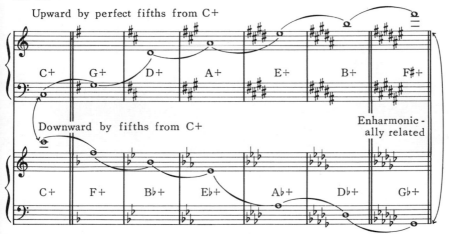

---

[5] Extension of the system leads to C-sharp major, with seven sharps; beyond this, double sharps appear in the key signature.

[6] Extension of the system leads to C-flat major with seven flats; beyond this, double flats appear in the key signature.

The same system is true of minor keys except that we start with the key of A minor, which, like C major, has no accidentals in its signature.

Ex. 81

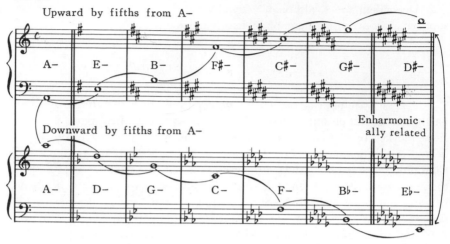

5

The Triad

The "Chord of Nature"

Each step of the scale possesses both melodic and chordal properties. Melodically, it forms horizontal associations with other tones; chordally, it forms vertical associations. Just which tones should enter into simple vertical relationships is indicated by the overtone series. As we have already seen, the fundamental-tone-overtone intervals that have their counterpart in the art of music extend to the fifth overtone. It is in this series of tones that the basis of vertical organization may be found. For purposes of convenient discussion, this chord of nature is reduced by the elimination of all duplicating tones and by contracting the range. The result is a three tone chord or triad.

Ex. 82

The Chord of Nature

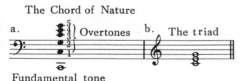

Fundamental tone

Minor and Diminished Triads

All musical tones have a natural tendency to express a similar triad. If, for example, we think of the tone D, the relationships it forms with its overtones are those illustrated in Example 83*a*, which may be reduced to those in Example 83*b*.

Ex. 83

As long as the tone D is considered by itself it is free to express its triad in this form. However, as soon as it becomes a member of a more inclusive group of tones, let us say the scale of C major, its natural rights may be exercised only as long as they offer no contradiction to the fundamental demand for complete agreement among the tones of the scale. The F–sharp in the D triad is contradicted by the fourth step, F, of C major; hence in the interests of the community of tones that express this scale, the F–sharp must be changed to F.

Ex. 84

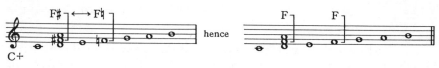

All triad tones that contradict the steps of the scale must be similarly altered. By thus sacrificing the vertical birthright of the second, third, sixth, and seventh steps a highly interrelated group of tones is won.

Ex. 85

a. Natural form of Triads

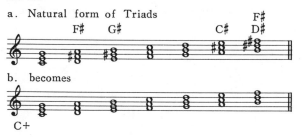

b. becomes

At the same time it can be pointed out that one of the great advantages of the major and minor scales is their flexibility and their ability to expand their relationships while retaining their identity. Examples of this were found in the discussion of mixed scales, where it was learned that C major remained C major even after the substitution of the minor scale forms of the sixth and seventh steps, A–flat and B–flat, for the original A and B. By the same token, as the harmonic relationships of C major are extended, the triads on occasion regain their natural form.

The triad that suffers most by this process of eliminating contradictory tones is that built on the seventh step, for two of its tones undergo alteration. Because this triad is two steps removed from its natural form, it is of all chords, the most difficult to use smoothly and convincingly.

THE NAMES OF TRIADS

When reference is made to the tones of the scale as melodic entities, Arabic numerals are used; when made to them as chords, Roman numerals are used. It is also customary to refer to the chords in terms of the names assigned to each degree of the scale. Thus we speak of the "two chord" or the "supertonic triad," and write it as "II," not as "2."

Ex. 86

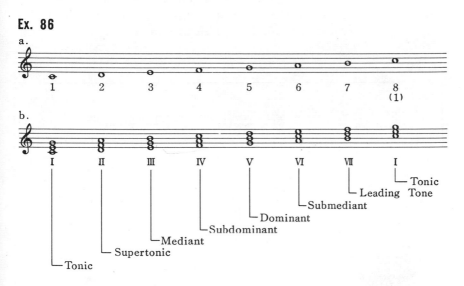

THE NAMES OF TRIAD TONES

The lowest tone in the natural arrangement of the triad, as well as in the more compact reduced arrangement, is called the root. This is the tone which suggested the triad through its overtones. The other tones are called the third and fifth, according to their interval distance from the root.

Ex. 87

The names that the triad tones acquire from this arrangement remain fixed regardless of how the triad may be expressed.

Ex. 88

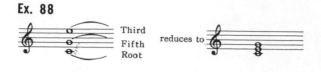

TRIAD QUALITIES

Triads have qualities just as intervals do. In the major mode there are three qualities, and a triad is one or another of them according to the quality of the intervals formed by its third and fifth with the root.

Ex. 89

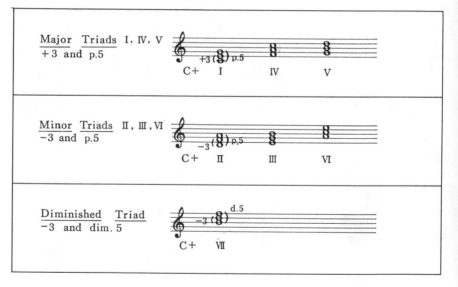

TRIAD POSITIONS

By inversion

Each of the tones that form a triad may appear as the *lowest* tone. As it does, it forms characterizing intervals with the tones above. It is by these intervals that the various positions are known. Hence, as indicated in Example 90, when C of the triad C-E-G is the lowest tone, it forms a fifth and a third with the tones above; consequently it is known as the *five-three position* (90a). When E is lowest, it forms a sixth and a third with the tones above, and is known as the *six-three position,* or in a shorter form, as the *position of the sixth* (90b). In the same manner, when G is lowest it forms the *six-four position* (90c). Observe, in Examples 90a, b, and c, that it is the lowest tone and the intervals it forms with the tones above that create each position. The distribution of the tones above plays no role in determining a position.

When positions are generated in this manner, by turning a chord about on itself, they are said to arise though *inversion.* The five-three position is called the root position, the position of the sixth is called the first inversion, and the six-four position, the second inversion.

By contrapuntal movement

Positions may also be created through melodic or contrapuntal motion. Note in Examples 90e and f that a melodic movement *away from* one or another triad tone creates the positions. A comparison of Example 90d with 90g will indicate the differences between positions by inversion and positions by contrapuntal movement.

The designation of each position remains the same regardless of the manner in which it is created, for it is interval content that characterizes each as five-three, six-three, or six-four. But the manner of generation (by inversion or by contrapuntal movement) is of critical importance to the study of harmony, as we shall see in the chapters to come. As always, the context in which a triad appears will be the determining factor.

Ex. 90

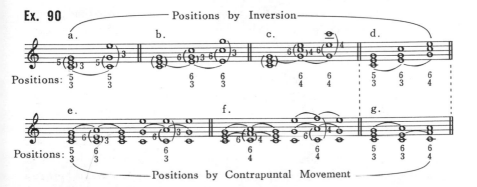

Positions by Inversion

Positions by Contrapuntal Movement

6

Chord Construction

THE NATURE AND PURPOSE OF EXERCISES

In understanding the principles of harmony, the first problems are those concerned with the construction of chords, the connection of chords or, voice leading, the clear expression of meter, and the organization of musical material in simple forms. Only by imposing certain restrictions upon the assigned exercises with regard to the medium of performance, the style to be employed, and the length can these four problems be met in their original and simplest terms. Exercises are to be regarded more as a testing ground preparatory to greater freedom than as examples of free composition, even though, when chorale tunes and folk melodies are harmonized, there seems to be a similarity to certain kinds of composition. The difference lies in the aim of such harmonizations, which is the exploitation of specific techniques rather than unrestricted indulgence in any of several settings that might fit just as well or perhaps even better. The musically mature composer is always free to select the precise form of expression he deems best suited to his purpose; the student of harmony is controlled in his choice with a view to establishing laboratory conditions where basic principles common to all styles of music may be subjected to experiment, where necessary distinctions between better and poorer ways of expression may be established. Only in this way can instruction be ordered and the foundations for thorough musicianship be laid.

The restricted nature of the singing voice when compared to the complexity that is possible in writing for instruments is the most certain guarantor of simplicity of expression. In writing for voices, first problems of chord construction and connection can be met in their original forms. The problems of instrumental music are largely derivative and superimposed on these. Hence, most exercises will be worked out for a vocal quartet consisting of a soprano, alto, tenor, and bass.

The arrangement of voices

The clearest compact way of arranging four such voices or parts is by using a great staff, the upper staff of which is reserved for the soprano and alto and the lower staff for the tenor and bass. Furthermore, to prevent confusion within each pair of voices, always point the soprano stems upward and the alto stems downward. Similarly in the bass clef point all tenor stems upward and all bass stems downward. Consult Example 91.

Ex. 91

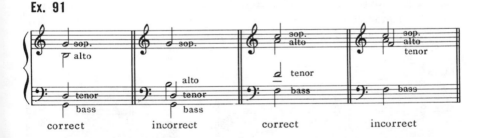

These practices should be observed even in those cases where voices cross.

Ex. 92

The range of each voice

The range of each voice in vocal exercises should be a normal, untaxing one, as charted in Example 93. The black notes indicate possible extensions. The upper and lower limits of each voice should be used sparingly.

Ex. 93

THREE RULES OF CHORD CONSTRUCTION

Of the four problems enumerated at the beginning of this chapter, the first involved the construction of chords. The demand for the best possible vertical arrangement of tones is most simply met when three rules are heeded.

1. Complete triad

Whenever possible all three tones of a triad should be used in its construction. This will make for explicitness. For purposes of smooth voice leading it is advisable on occasion to omit the fifth of the triad, but the root which gives the chord its identity and the third, without which the chord sounds empty, are indispensable. See Example 94.

Ex. 94

2. Doubling of tones

In order to express a three tone chord in four voices, one of the tones has to be duplicated or doubled. The choice of the tone to double often rests with the demands of good voice leading; but other things being equal, it is best to follow the order of Nature[1] by doubling the root. Second best is to double the fifth and least good is to double the third. However, do not double the leading tone of the scale when it is in the V or VII chords. In other words, do not double the third of the V or the root of the VII. The reason for this prohibition is that the leading tone, by virtue of its active melodic character which is emphasized when it is associated with these two chords, stands out sufficiently without being doubled. Doubling it can easily ruin the balance of the chord. As the fifth of the III chord, the leading tone may be doubled. See Example 95.

Ex. 95

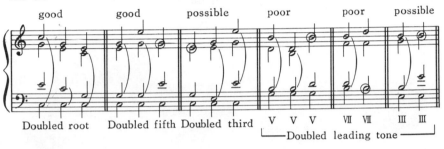

3. Good spacing

An excessively large interval between adjacent upper tones may produce a thin, poorly arranged chord. Avoid this by placing the voices in such a way that the alto lies no more than an octave from both the tenor and soprano. Occasional difficulties of voice leading may best be solved by exceeding this octave limit, but such situations arise rarely and can usually be circumvented. The tenor and bass may be separated by two octaves without damage to the sound of the chord.

Ex. 96

[1] See Ex. 82a.

These three rules calling for a complete triad, proper doubling, and good spacing will assure satisfactory vertical organization. Each one of them is subject to modification by the demands of fluent voice leading or horizontal motion. It will become evident through experience that usually the horizontal and the vertical work hand in hand. Situations arise, however, in which the perfection of one must be sacrificed to the improvement of the other. In most of these cases the smooth flow of parts should receive first consideration. The best solution to an exercise is that which maintains a fine balance between the two directions, vertical and horizontal, and allows neither to suffer from undue attention paid to the other.

A summary of this material appears at the end of Chapter 7.

7

Voice Leading

The Twofold Nature of Voice Leading

The second of the problems enumerated at the beginning of Chapter 6 was voice leading. As we have already seen, chord construction is concerned with the vertical arrangement of tones. Voice leading has to do with the horizontal succession of tones, with the melodic nature of voices. Each voice may be considered as it exists by itself or as it forms interval relationships with other voices. Both of these aspects of moving parts are the concern of voice leading.

The Single Voice

The function of each voice

In writing a four-part exercise, it must be remembered that each voice has its special function. The soprano part, as the upper-most voice, is the most important melodically, and to it should be given the most attractive and interesting line. The bass interprets and gives exact meaning to the numerous harmonic implications of the soprano. For instance, in Example 97 the motion B-C suggests several possible chords.

Ex. 97

The bass by its motion determines which of these is to be used and in doing so is at times obliged to suffer melodically. The two remaining voices, the tenor and alto, have as their chief function the filling in of the tones of the chords and the dispelling of any vestige of doubt as to their identity. They should do this unobtrusively. Dull alto and tenor parts do not make a dull exercise. On the other hand, a monotonous soprano may very easily prove ruinous.

Ex. 98

To illustrate these remarks let us examine the first four bars of Bach's setting of "Werde munter, mein Gemüthe." The alto and tenor parts are not exactly epoch-making melodies, and the bass concentrates its attention more on indicating the succession of chords than on the creation of a suave melodic line. At the same time the effect of the whole is completely satisfying and interesting.

Ex. 99

This distribution of functions simplifies the tasks of chord construction and voice leading. For the time being the inner voices should be completely subordinated to the melodic flow of the soprano and the harmonic activity of the bass. Later, with the introduction of tones of figuration, it will become possible for the alto and tenor, as well as the bass, to free themselves some-what from bondage and to assume increasing rhythmic and melodic impor-tance, thereby adding to the interest of the exercise. The opening bars of Bach's setting of "Herr Jesu Christ, wahr'r Mensch und Gott" are a good example of a freely moving tenor and bass. The two voices are engaged not solely in their primary missions of indicating the progression of chords and completing them but also in the expression of independent rhythmic and thematic relationships. Note particularly how the eighth note motion F-G-A, etc. in the bass is answered by the tenor's C-D-E, etc. In fact, it is the pursuit of this imitation that brings about and justifies the doubling, including a doubled seventh step on the third beat of the first bar.

Ex. 100

Conjunct and disjunct motions

Each voice may move by conjunct or disjunct motion. When the interval from one tone of a melody to another is a second, the motion is conjunct or stepwise; when the interval is larger than a second, the motion is disjunct. After the repeated tone the simplest and most easily sung motions are the conjunct motions of a major and a minor second.[1] Of disjunct motions the easiest to sing are the consonant skips. The most difficult are the dissonant skips. In constructing each part, give preference to the simplest progression; that is, repeat tones whenever possible, move by conjunct motion when there is no opportunity to repeat a tone, and only when conjunct motion leads to undesirable relationships with other voices use disjunct motion, giving preference to consonant over dissonant skips. Example 101 tabulates a series of diatonic progressions from the easier to the more difficult to sing.

Ex. 101   Table of single voice motions

1. Repeated tone

2. Conjunct motion

[1] For the time being, and until Ch. 15 is reached, the augmented second will be excluded from use. It represents conjunct motion in name only.

Ex. 101 (cont'd)

Table of single voice motions (cont'd)

3. Disjunct motion

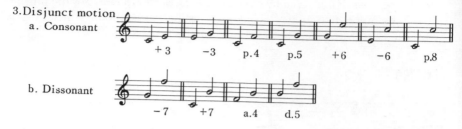

As our repertoire of chords grows in complexity, it will be possible to make more frequent use of the difficult disjunct motions.[2] A word must be said about the bass which, in indicating simple harmonic progressions, is sometimes obliged to leap from tone to tone much more than the other voices. Until all positions of chords have been discussed it will be impossible to do very much to alter this condition.

The voice leading in Example 102a is inferior to that of Example 102b because the parts, particularly the soprano, are unnecessarily awkward and complex in construction.

Ex. 102

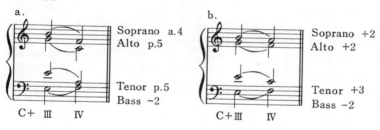

a.

Soprano a.4
Alto p.5

Tenor p.5
Bass −2

C+ III   IV

b.

Soprano +2
Alto +2

Tenor +3
Bass −2

C+III   IV

THE RELATIONSHIP OF VOICES TO EACH OTHER

Voice leading, as we have seen, is concerned not only with the melodic progressions of a single voice but also with the relationships between two or more voices in motion. Three kinds of composite motion are possible between two voices, the last of which exists in two forms, as shown in Example 103.

[2] Specifically, in Ch. 15.

Ex. 103

a. Contrary Motion

b. Oblique Motion

c.1 Similar Motion

c.2 Parallel Motion

Two ideals should be kept in mind in working out exercises. First, the voices should prove that they belong together. This is the task of chord construction or vertical relationship. The fact that each voice participates in the expression of chords is token enough of a common interest. Secondly, the voices should prove that they possess individuality and are not completely dependent on each other for their existence. This is the task of voice leading or horizontal motion. Of the three composite voice motions, the best adapted to creating independence is contrary motion, for here the voices repudiate each other in coming together or in moving apart. Oblique motion is the next best in that the inactivity of one voice is contradicted by the activity of the other. The least satisfactory are parallel and similar motions in which voices move in the same direction. Similar motion is somewhat better than parallel motion inasmuch as the change in the size of the intervals is at least a gesture toward individuality.

Forbidden parallel motions

Not all parallel motions are bad, but some so completely deny independence of motion that they should not be used when the aim is the construction of individually alive parts.

1. The first of these poor motions is *parallel motion in unisons*. Here, obviously, the two voices are completely merged into one compound voice.

Ex. 104

2. The second faulty motion is *parallel motion in octaves*. The octave, as we have seen, is nothing more than a duplication of a single sound in another register, and this is enough to destroy independent part writing.

Ex. 105

3. The third faulty motion is *parallel motion in perfect fifths*. The reason for prohibiting this kind of parallel motion is that tones lying a perfect fifth apart form the closest possible relationship that exists between tones of different pitch-names.[3] Hence parallel motion in perfect fifths is to be avoided because such a motion identifies voices too closely to be in keeping with our plans for independence of parts.

Ex. 106

EXCLUSIONS FROM "PARALLEL RULES"

Thus the prohibited motions are those in parallel unisons, octaves, and perfect fifths. This rule will be more clearly understood when consideration is given to certain relationships to which it does not apply.

1. One perfect unison, octave, or fifth is not bad.

---

[3] Review the section, *The Partial Tone Series and Music*, Ch. 1.

Ex. 107

2. Repeated unisons, octaves, or fifths are not bad, for no motion is involved. The difference between a repeated tone and a held tone is not one of principle but one of execution.

Ex. 108

3. Only when one and the same pair of voices creates the parallel motion is it prohibited. Examples 109a and c are incorrect; the others are quite satisfactory.

Ex. 109

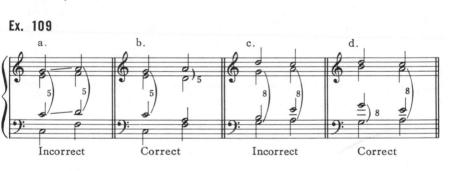

Incorrect   Correct   Incorrect   Correct

4. If one of the fifths is diminished, the progression is acceptable. However, when the diminished fifth is the first of the pair as in Example 110c and d, the attending circumstances must justify the melodic circumvention of, in example c, the tone E, to which the F would normally progress, and in example d, of the tone C, to which the B would normally progress.[4] In any event, the "parallel rule" does not apply when one fifth is diminished.

Ex. 110

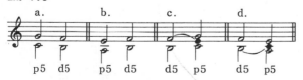

p5   d5   p5   d5   d5   p5   d5   p5

[4] Review Ex. 8.

5. Not all parallel motions are bad. In fact, it is needless and in many cases impossible always to avoid parallel or similar motions. The connection of any two chords will inevitably involve one or both of the motions, as in Example 111.

Ex. 111

C+   I   V

6. Furthermore, parallel motion in thirds or sixths is extremely useful on those occasions when two voices unite in performing a common task, as in the alto and tenor parts of Bach's "Meinen Jesum lass' ich nicht":

Ex. 112

ILLUSTRATIONS

A few simple illustrations will suffice to demonstrate the manner in which the two aspects of voice leading control the motions of parts in chord successions. If in the succession I-V-I the soprano starts on C, it may continue its motion by moving to B and back to C, or by moving to D and then to either C or E, as in Example 113.

Ex. 113

C+   I   V   I   I   V   I

Any other soprano motions starting from C involve, for our purposes, unnecessary skips or the use of tones that do not express the stated succession of chords. The inner voices encounter no difficulty in filling out the chords when the soprano sings C-B-C. In Example 114a the tenor, starting on G, repeats it through the remaining chords and the alto, starting on E, moves by stepwise motion to D and back to E again. These motions are interchanged in example b. Not only is the voice leading satisfactory but the chords are also all well constructed.

Ex. 114

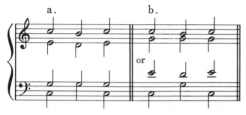

Difficulties arise in the middle voices when the soprano motion is C-D-E. A skip is necessary in order to win complete chords. Several ways of completing the progression are shown in Example 115.

Ex. 115

In Example 115c, the fifth of the second chord is doubled and the last chord is incomplete. Compare this with Examples d and f, where a complete final chord is won by denying the melodic tendency of the seventh step to progress to the tonic degree.[5] This happens frequently when the seventh step is in an inner voice where the denial of its normal melodic motion is covered by the other voices; it rarely happens when it is in the soprano where its melodic nature comes to the fore. In Example f the spacing of the alto and soprano exceeds the usual limit of an octave. Spacing such as this should be used only when an ensuing skip conveniently restores the normal distances between the voices as in Example 116.

[5] See the alto of the final two chords, Ex. 99.

Ex. 116

Compare Example 115*f* with 115*g*, in which the alto skips a fourth to maintain good spacing. As a result of this skip the alto and the bass in the second and third chords lie a perfect fifth apart. Since the voices move by opposite motion these fifths do not violate the parallel-fifths rule. Solutions similar to those of Example 115 are possible when the soprano motion is C-D-C as in Example 117.

Ex. 117

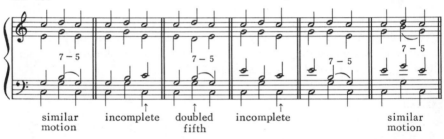

similar   incomplete   doubled   incomplete   similar
motion   fifth   motion

In the succession IV-V, in fact in any succession involving roots that are a second apart, care must be exercised to avoid parallel unisons, octaves, and fifths. Example 118 illustrates good and poor ways of connecting such chords.

Ex. 118

a. poor   b. good   c. poor   d. poor   e. poor   f. good

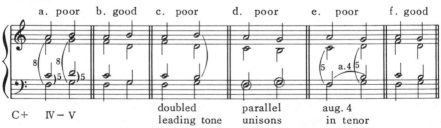

C+   IV – V   doubled   parallel   aug. 4
                          leading tone   unisons   in tenor

Occasionally a good distribution of parts in the first chord will create difficulties as the parts move to succeeding chords. Compare Example 119*a* with 119*b*. The tenor, spaced satisfactorily at the beginning of the connection in Example *a*, becomes awkward near the end. The voice leading is smoother in Example *b*. Compare the two opening arrangements under *a* and *b* in Example 119.

Ex. 119

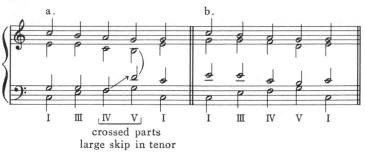

From this example it can be seen that it is a good practice to keep the tenor and alto high, especially when the bass ascends. For one thing, such an arrangement of inner parts will eliminate a crossing of lower voices or an alternative introduction of a wide leap. For another, it will create a more convenient arrangement of parts when exercises are played at the keyboard; the three upper parts are usually played by the right hand and the bass by the left alone. The divided performance, with bass and tenor played by the left hand, and alto and soprano by the right, is more difficult and less frequent.

SUMMARY OF CHAPTERS 6 AND 7

The material covered in this and the preceding chapter can be summarized conveniently as follows:

1. Chord construction.
    a. Use a complete chord when possible; omit the fifth if necessary.
    b. Double the root. If this is impossible, double the fifth. As a last resort double the third. Avoid a doubled leading tone in the V and VII.
    c. Do not place adjacent upper voices more than an octave apart.
2. Voice leading.
    a. Repeat tones when possible. Give preference to conjunct motion over disjunct. In disjunct motion use consonant rather than dissonant leaps.
    b. Avoid parallel unisons, octaves, and perfect fifths.
    c. In general, keep the inner parts high.

8

Chord Succession—
Root Position

In this chapter and several of those that follow we shall describe the ways in which chords succeed each other to create a convincing musical continuity. Our concern will be directed not only to chord succession but just as much to the closely related problem of chord selection. Many factors influence the choosing of one chord rather than another in a given situation; some of these are personal and others are related to the particular musical style of an exercise. But the factors whose study will prove most profitable here have to do with basic principles of succession. For one thing, it is apparent that no chord can be selected without reference to its place in a context, in a broader pattern of chords. Our first task is always to locate the context in which our chords are to fit. Because chordal contexts are similar to those that form melodic continuity, we shall use the terms principal and dependent here just as we did in analyzing melodies. *Principal chords* are those that mark the limits and important points of a passage; *dependent chords* are those that take us from one to another principal chord. More specifically, dependent chords help to create a flowing bass, to correct awkward voice leading, and to accompany dependent melodic tones. Often these functions are exercised simultaneously. For example, a chord that harmonizes a passing tone can, at the same time, make the bass more melodic or eliminate poor voice leading.

Chords are related to each other harmonically according to the distance between their roots. The strongest and most binding relationship occurs when the roots lie a perfect fifth or fourth apart, as in the progression V-I. We shall open our discussion by examining this kind of progression, which is based on a natural harmonic principle. Other chordal relationships are concerned with roots which are separated by a third or sixth (I-VI), and a second or seventh (IV-V). These progressions are often by-products of the natural succession by fifths as we shall see presently.

The student is thus armed with two complementary sets of operating principles when he turns his attention to chord succession or selection. First, he must know what his chord is going to do, he must be able to describe its function as principal or dependent. Second, he must be able to identify his chord properly and relate its root to other surrounding roots. In brief, a chord is known by its behavior and its identity. As we proceed with our study it will become apparent that behavior is often more significant than root identity, especially where dependent chords are concerned.

ROOT PROGRESSION BY FIFTHS

The natural succession

The most fundamental principle of harmonic motion is based on the strong relationship of tones that lie a perfect fifth apart.[1] Harmonically, each chord root in the major scale progresses readily to those roots that lie a perfect fifth above or a perfect fifth below it. Thus, the harmonic form of the scale is quite different in appearance from the melodic form.

Ex. 120

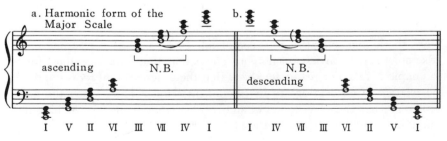

a. Harmonic form of the Major Scale

    b.

ascending   N.B.

    N.B. descending

I V II VI III VII IV I   I IV VII III VI II V I

There is a point in Example 120 where the major scale in its harmonic form departs from a succession of perfect fifths, at the place where VII moves to IV, and also in reverse, where IV moves to VII. Both are marked N.B. in the example. In this hazardous area (IV, VII, III), the root progression of a diminished fifth is not easy to execute. Adding to the difficulty

---

[1] As discussed in Ch. 1.

is the diminished quality of VII. Both of these challenges will be discussed later in this chapter under *The VII.*

All traditional diatonic scales, often called the "ecclesiastical modes," contain the same diminished fifth. As noted earlier, it is the major mode alone that turns this deficiency to distinct key-defining advantage because of the position, on the seventh and fourth steps, of the diminished fifth, once called "the devil in music."[2]

Four part settings of the natural succession

To turn this natural relationship to musical use, that is, to bring the succession into accord with principles of voice leading and the limitations of the singing voice, certain of the fifths from one root to another have to be inverted, as can be seen by studying the bass of Example 121. Allowing for the weakness of that part of the harmonic form of the scale that centers about the VII, the form that the two progressions I-V-II-VI-III-VII-IV-I and I-IV-VII-III-VI-II-V-I take when arranged for four voices appears in Example 121.[3]

Ex. 121

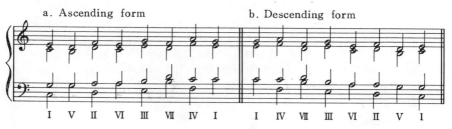

When the harmonic scale is thus completely expressed, the descending form (Example 121*b*) carries much more conviction than the ascending form (Example 121*a*). The reason for this is that the progression of roots stands in the relation of an overtone to its fundamental tone. Thus, when the final tonic is reached the effect is that of an overtone (root of the V) reaching the final fundamental tone (root of the I):

---

[2] Review, in Ch. 2, *Melodically active half step relationships,* and *The leading tone.* Also, in Ch. 4, *Key defining intervals, major mode,* and *Key defining intervals, minor mode.*

[3] Compare Ex. 121 with 120.

Ex. 122

In the ascending form just the opposite is the case: the final I is in effect like an overtone of the IV, hence less clear in its finality:

Ex. 123

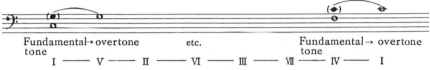

Partial uses of the natural succession

The practical results of these relationships are far-reaching. For one thing, it can be established immediately that any chord can be succeeded readily by those whose roots lie a perfect fifth above or below it. We must keep in mind that as this principle is applied it is sometimes to the advantage of the setting to move the root a perfect fourth downward instead of a perfect fifth upward. Regardless of whether the succession of roots is by perfect fifths or their inversion, perfect fourths, the harmonic result will be the same. For example:

Ex. 124

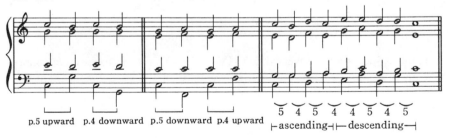

Thus, the II moves persuasively to either the VI whose root lies a perfect fifth above or to the V whose root lies a perfect fifth below. To show its harmonic relationship to the I, however, it progresses by descending fifths through the V to the I:

Ex. 125

C+   II — VI   II — V   II — V — I

This principle is true of every chord in the key, with the reservation that the least dependable part of the harmonic scale embraces III-VII-IV, as we have seen.

I-IV-V-I

On consulting the harmonic form of the scale, it becomes evident that the most frequently expressed chords, I, IV, and V, lie at the beginning and end of the natural succession. In fact, these three chords alone form a compact way of expressing any key harmonically. Starting downward by fifths, I-IV, a connection can by established directly with V-I. Thus the two ends of the system may be joined, as in Example 126.

Ex. 126

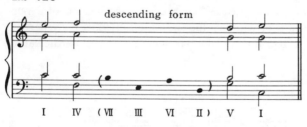

I   IV   (VII   III   VI   II)   V   I

When this succession is reversed, I-V-IV-I, the IV in most cases sounds more like an interpolation than an essential member of the progression (Example 127).

Ex. 127

I — V —(IV) — I   I — V — I

Because I-V-IV-I is always subject to a special interpretation, it is not as fundamental and guiding a progression as I-IV-V-I.

Summary

1. The complete natural succession of triads in a key is best realized in the descending progression I-IV-VII-III-VI-II-V-I.

2. Any triad in a key moves naturally to the triad whose root lies a fifth above it and to the triad whose root lies a fifth below it. To reach the I naturally from any chord move by descending fifths.

3. The three primary chords are I, IV, and V.

Roots That Lie a Third Apart

Associate triads

Certain recurrent situations of voice leading may be conveniently summarized by establishing an association between chords whose roots lie a third apart. There are many applications of this relationship. In its most frequently used form the tonic, subdominant and dominant chords—those that carry most of the harmonic activity expressive of a key—have as associates the remaining triads, as shown in Example 128. A reason for this association can be found in the fact that there are always two tones in common between triads whose roots lie a third apart.

Ex. 128

Primary Triads	Associate Triads	
	VI	
I	III	
	II	
IV	VI (occasionally)	

Ex. 128   (cont'd)

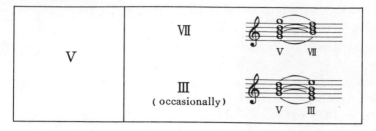

Uses of associate triads

All of the progressions that grow out of Example 128 can be understood best in terms of a more inclusive framework of chords. Associate chords usually occupy themselves with some smaller detail of harmonization. To evaluate their usefulness in a given situation, criteria that stress context and horizontal motion must be used. In the following examples, associate chords perform one function or another in a progression whose total plan involves the connection of roots a fifth apart, such as I-V or I-IV.

1. Between chord roots a fifth apart. In the progression I-IV, the descending fifth in the bass may be broken up into two thirds by interpolating the VI. Compare the bass in Example 129a with that in Example b.

Ex. 129

The VI is, in such a case, a dependent chord, a detail of harmonic motion. Observe the use of parentheses to indicate this in the harmonic analysis of Example 129.

This employment of roots a third apart may be applied to other connections: as in Example 130, in moving from VI to II the IV may be inserted as a dependent chord:

Ex. 130

2. *The harmonization of dependent tones.* The chord whose root lies a third above that of a principal chord is often a result of a particular solution of a problem of voice leading. Example 131*a* illustrates a connection involving the I and IV, with the bass ascending a fourth. Note how the passing tone B forms a dissonance with the root of the I. By using the tone E in the bass as in Example *b,* this dissonance is changed into a consonance. Thus the III chord is formed as a vertical result of a technique of voice leading, the transformation of an originally dissonant relationship into a consonant one.[4]

Ex. 131

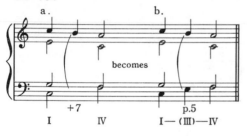

The same technique may be used in an identical situation involving the progression II-V as shown in Example 132.[5]

---

[4] Review Ch. 4, *Melodic Attributes of Intervals.*

[5] The succession usually sounds awkward when VII (a dissonant triad to start with and not a good "transformer") is part of it, as in IV-(VI)-VII, V-(VII)-I, and VII-(II)-III. The remaining usable transpositions are III-(V)-VI and VI-(I)-II.

Ex. 132

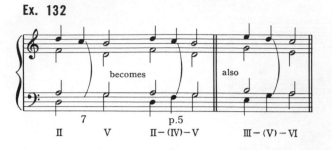

ROOTS THAT LIE A SECOND APART

As by-products

Progressions of chords whose roots lie a second apart often arise as incidents of other techniques. Examine Examples 126 (I-IV-V-I), 127 (I-V-IV-I), 131*b* (I-III-IV), and 132 (II-IV-V). Progressions by seconds are also a result of the replacement of the IV in the succession I-IV-V-I by its associate chord, the II (Example 133).

Ex. 133

The progression also arises when, in the succession I-V, the VI is interpolated as an associate of the I to fill in the bass.

Ex. 134

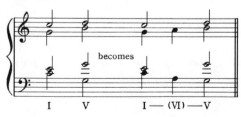

As neighbors

The progression of roots a second apart is often the result of a neighboring tone motion in the bass. Note in Example 135 how the bass and soprano mirror one another's neighboring tone motion.

Ex. 135

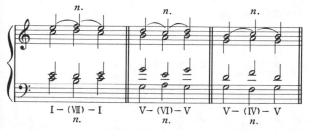

So far, the harmonic nature of the connection of roots a fifth apart, the association between chords whose roots lie a third apart, and the incidental nature of progressions involving roots a second apart have been discussed. The examples of voice leading techniques have illustrated the insertion of a chord to fill in the bass line [I-(VI)-IV or I-(VI)-V], and the harmonization of dependent tones [I-(III)-IV and I-(VII)-I]. In most of the illustrations the extent of activity was the interval of a fifth or its inversion, the fourth, in the bass.

Additional Illustrations

The harmonization of dependent tones

The problem in moving to associate chords in the following examples concerns finding a bass tone and consequently another chord to harmonize the dissonant passing tone. The problem is identical with that of Examples 131 and 132, except that the total plan now involves roots a third, and its inversion, a sixth, apart. In Example 136, the threat of parallel octaves and fifths is avoided by the interpolated chord.

Ex. 136

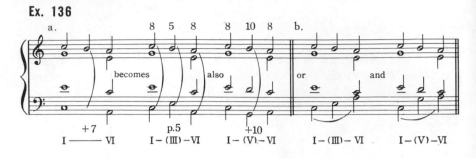

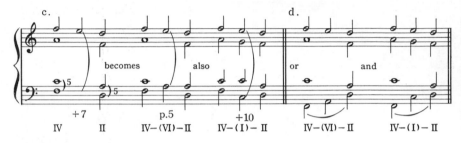

The same technique gives rise to new chords when the total plan is to traverse a second in the bass, as in Example 137.

Ex. 137

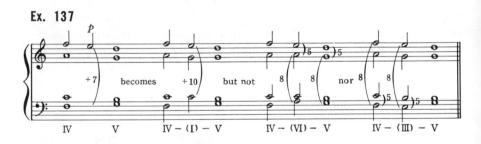

Corrective chords

In certain connections between roots a second apart, an inserted chord is necessary to break up parallel octaves and fifths (Example 138).

Ex. 138

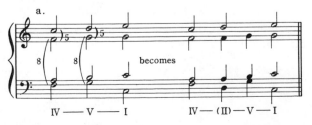

b.

c.

d.

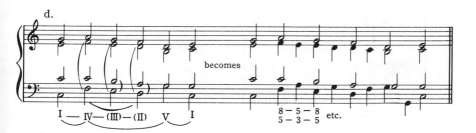

e.

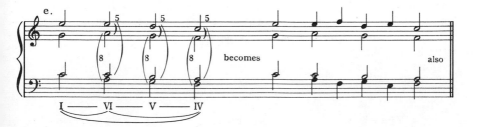

The same kind of insertion is necessary under certain melodic conditions to avert parallel octaves and fifths when the bass moves by thirds (Example 139).

Ex. 139

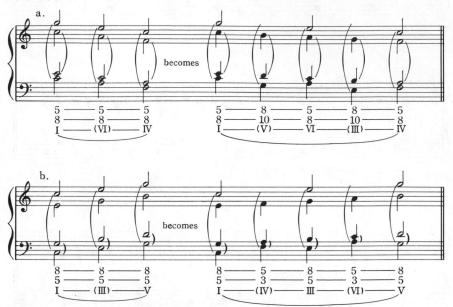

It should be apparent from this discussion that in such work of detail the step names of the inserted chords are of no importance. The motivating force is the interval relationships between voices as they move from one point to another. The chords are born out of voice leading. Their root names are the result of motion and not the originating force.

The VII

The VII in root position is a treacherous chord to use because of the thin sound of its diminished fifth. It has appeared in only Examples 121 *a* and *b,* and 135. The deficiencies of its sound can be reduced to a minimum when the third, the tone that plays no role in the formation of the diminished fifth, is doubled.

Ex. 140

VII
doubled third

Also, the diminished fifth formed by the outer voices should resolve to a major third.

Ex. 141

4 —→ 3

7 —→ 8
d.5 → +3

The one exception to this is in the natural succession VII-III, where only the fourth step of the scale (the fifth of the VII) moves in the prescribed manner.

Ex. 142

4　　3

VII — III

Furthermore, emphasis should be placed on contextual nature by introducing with stepwise motion either one or both of the tones that create its diminished fifth.

Ex. 143

I — (VII) — I　　　I — (VII) — I　　　V — (VII) — I
d.5 → +3　　　　　d.5 → +3　　　　　d.5 → +3

When the chord fifth is common to the preceding chord, the meagerness of the diminished fifth is offset by the smoothness of its entrance.

Ex. 144

Whenever such conditions are lacking in the use of the VII it is best to consider the possibility of using another chord that labors under no such restrictions.

CONCLUSION

All of the examples in this chapter have been fragmentary. They represent nothing more than details which, to make sense, have to be heard as sections of more extensive progressions. Most of the chords that we hear in music are products of voice leading; they carry out some horizontal function. These are the dependent chords. They take on meaning only as our ears consult their immediate context. The more stable chords, those that govern motion and that have larger, more inclusive contexts, are the principal chords.

9

Exercises

INTRODUCTION

To develop harmonic skill, three kinds of exercises will be used: figured basses, chord drills, and the harmonizing of melodies. These will be executed primarily in four part vocal style, as discussed in Chapter 6. From time to time a restricted keyboard style will be employed. Three part assignments will be made on occasion. The value of such exercises is that each stresses particular aspects of musical experience.

FIGURED BASS EXERCISES

The figured bass requires the constructing of a well-phrased, meaningful soprano and the working out of problems of voice leading. The chords are always given in such exercises and are to be regarded as final. Problems of chord selection and succession are not present here. At the same time progressions that might not occur readily to the student may be learned through a figured bass.

There are several ways of indicating that a given tone in the bass is to be regarded as the root of a chord. Since the upper tones are a fifth and a third above the root, the numerals $\frac{5}{3}$ may be placed under the given tone. Sometimes only one of the numerals is used; sometimes, none.

Ex. 145

Figured bass indications
of root position

The numerals are not to be construed as indicating the distribution of the tones of the chord. When $\frac{5}{3}$ appears under a bass tone, it does not mean that the soprano must be given only the fifth of the chord; it may happen that the soprano according to its connection with the preceding and following chords could better be given the third or the root. Again, the third and fifth of the chord may appear in any register convenient to the horizontal situation. Hence $\frac{5}{3}$, 5, 3, or no numeral indicates that a triad in root position is to be used, but not how it is to be used. Example 146 indicates a few of the ways in which a figured tone may be expressed.

Ex. 146

In working out a figured bass exercise, construct the soprano before filling in the middle parts. Avoid monotonous repetitions and chaotic leaps. Try to shape the soprano so that it works toward a definite point; whether the point is higher or lower than the beginning is of little moment so long as the soprano moves with conviction. After the soprano has been constructed, fill in the inner parts. A good and a poor realization of the figured bass in Example 147*a* are illustrated in *b* and *c*. While both constructions are free of errors of voice leading, *b* with its dull soprano is meaningless.

Ex. 147

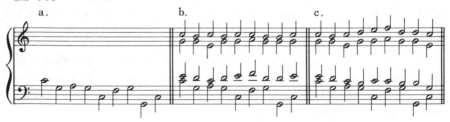

THE CHORD DRILL

A second kind of exercise, the chord drill, has as its purpose the rehearsing of techniques of voice leading and chord succession under various situations with regard to the soprano and bass. These exercises are always short and fragmentary with the emphasis placed on the simplest way of executing the assigned successions. The drills prepare the way for the more complex problems that arise in figured basses and harmonizations. Whenever a soprano must be constructed in these exercises, it should be made to move simply and directly without thought of variety or arresting progressions.

THE HARMONIZATION OF MELODIES

The procedure

Our purpose in harmonizing melodies is to study the ways in which the upper voice exercises a general directive control over the selection of a bass and chords. Many bad harmonizations of a given melody are possible, but there is usually more than one good one. In order to eliminate as many of the bad as possible, one maxim must be adopted: Work from the general to the particular. Or, to put it negatively, do not set about harmonizing a melody by putting a chord under each successive note of the soprano. A thorough and dependable procedure may be summarized as follows:

I. Analyze the melody.
  a. Determine the key.
  b. Mark off the sections, phrases, and rhythmic groups.
  c. Locate the principal and dependent tones.
II. Sketch in the bass.
  a. Establish the cadences.
  b. Put bass tones under the principal melodic tones.
  c. Put bass tones under the dependent tones.
III. Fill in the middle voices.

Melodic analysis

Melodic analysis has already been discussed.[1] All that need be added now is that good harmonizations must agree with and validate the structural details of the melody. The tones that are analyzed as principal tones should receive first consideration harmonically. Just as principal tones are stable and guide melodic activity, so will the principal chords that harmonize them be stable and guide harmonic activity and voice leading. There is, in short, direct correlation between the two. They represent different ways of viewing the same idea. Example 148 is an analysis of a short melody, the harmoniza-

[1] Review in Ch. 2, *Melodic Analysis,* and in Ch. 4, *Melodic Attributes of Intervals.*

tion of which will serve to illustrate our adopted procedure. The key is F major. Formally, the melody divides into two parts, *A* and *B*, the division coming at the end of the second bar. In phrase *A* there is a passing tone, B-flat, in bar 1, and a complete neighbor, D, in bar 2. In phrase *B* there is a passing tone, G, in bar 3 and an incomplete neighbor, B-flat, followed by a passing tone, G, in the last measure.[2]

Ex. 148

The bass

1. Cadences. Our problem is now to construct a bass that agrees with this analysis. First, with regard to the form: Harmonically we are in need of some definite technique that will serve to reinforce the melodic halts at the end of bars two and four. The clearest way of doing this is by leading up to one of the three chords I, IV, and V, which are closest to the key center. Such a progression is called a *cadence*. Cadences fall into two general groups, complete and incomplete. *Complete cadences* are those in which the final chord is the tonic. This chord is always reached, at cadences, in the most persuasive way via the natural harmonic route; that is, it is preceded by either of those chords whose root lies a fifth away, the V or the IV. More frequently it is the V for the reason that was stated during the discussion of the natural harmonic relationship of roots a fifth apart.[3] The cadence V-I grows in conviction when a third (antepenultimate) chord, II, IV, or occasionally VI, precedes the V. The complete cadences involving **V-I**

Ex. 149

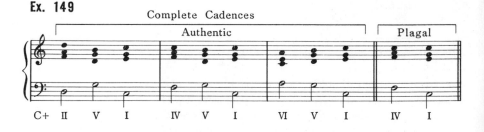

---

[2] Review Ex. 7*d*.
[3] Review in Ch. 8, *Root Progression by Fifths.*

as essential members are called authentic; those involving IV-I are called plagal. The soprano is variable but the bass is not.

Incomplete cadences are those that end on the IV or V, one harmonic degree away from the tonic. With these may be included the *deceptive cadence* in which the final chord is usually VI, as a substitute for I. The name deceptive arises from the fact that the antecedent chords in the cadence are so arranged that we expect the I; the intrusion of the VI literally "deceives" our ears.

Ex. 150

The harmonic cadences that may be applied to the melody we are harmonizing are illustrated below.

Ex. 151

2. *The harmonization of principal tones.* Harmonically, the formal, cadential requirements of the melody have been satisfied. Our next task is to take care of the broad harmonic implications of the rest of the melody. The activity of the principal tones C-A-C in the first phrase expresses nothing more than a tonic triad.

Ex. 152

The essential correctness of this bass can be tested by playing the melody against it.

Ex. 153

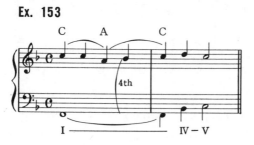

3. The harmonization of dependent tones. As pointed out during the discussion of consonance and dissonance, dependent tones may be harmonized or left unharmonized. The one place where free choice is restricted is at cadences, where there is a formal demand for harmonic activity. At a later time attention will be directed to unharmonized dependent tones. Here the task is to provide all tones with a bass and chord in root position. The dependent tones that are harmonized take on an added weight because of the support they receive from the bass.

The passing tone B–flat, in bar 1 of the first phrase, is in need of a harmonizing root in the bass. The other dependent tone, D, in bar 2 has been provided for by the cadence. This B–flat may be considered the root of a triad, which would give us B-flat in the bass and a IV, or the third of a triad which would make G the bass as the root of the II, or the fifth of a triad with E in the bass as the root of the VII.

Ex. 154

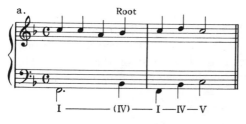

Of these three possible bass tones the IV is harmonically closest by fifths to the I; the II, whose root forms a neighboring tone to F in the bass, is a possible choice; but the unresolved diminished fifth in the outer voices of the VII makes it the poorest choice of all.

4. The elaboration of the bass. The safest choice is the harmonically close IV. Limiting ourselves to this harmonization for the present, we might proceed directly to the completion of the first phrase by filling in the inner voices. Details can be contrived to improve the contour of the bass. For example, if the first F in the bass is placed an octave higher, there will be an opportunity to break the fifth between it and B–flat by inserting D at the point where the melody reaches A:[4]

Ex. 155

This unfortunately creates parallel fifths. These may be avoided by a C in the bass under the second C in the soprano, which interpolates an octave between the fifths.[5]

---

[4] Review Ex. 128, 129, 130.
[5] Review Ex. 139*a*.

Ex. 156

I — V — VI

Let us restore the first F to its original register. This will create a sixth instead of the original third between it and D, which may be bridged by A in the bass.[6]

Ex. 157

I — (III) — (VI) — IV

These experiments might also be tried on the other setting of this phrase in which the II with G in the bass appeared instead of the IV with B–flat. The same procedure will prove fruitful with the second phrase.

5. The metric nature of the bass. The bass has one particular accentual duty to perform. By its motion more than by the motion of the upper voices, it reveals conformity with the meter. One awkward repetition may confuse this function: the repetition of a tone from a weak to a strong beat. The effect is that the bass arrives too soon at its destination.

Ex. 158

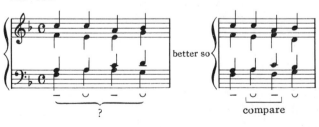

better so

?   compare

---

6 Review Ex. 136*b, d.*

To avoid this pitfall, change one of the tones.

On the other hand, repetitions in the bass from a strong to a weak beat are acceptable.

Ex. 159

Repetitions from a strong beat to a strong beat are good. Here, the effect of an included weak-strong repetition is not confusing because our ears hear the repetition from its inception on a strong beat and carry through the intervening weak beat to the next strong beat.

Ex. 160

In short, repetitions in the bass that start on a strong beat are good regardless of the extent of the repetition. Repeated tones in the bass starting on a weak beat are suspect.

The anacrusis. At a later time a study will be made of the conditions under which weak-strong repetitions operate successfully. For the present only one such case demands our attention. Phrases that start with an anacrusis (up beat) are rhythmically characterized by a motion from a weak beat to a strong beat.

Ex. 161

In this case the bass agrees with the rhythmic construction of the melody when it repeats from the weak beat to the first strong beat.

Ex. 162

Such an arrangement puts the burden of indicating the first strong metric pulse on the performer, for a slipshod noncommittal playing of the first two beats may create doubts as to which is the stronger.

Ex. 163

An upward octave skip in the bass makes the succession of beats much clearer, as does a change of bass tone over the bar.

Ex. 164

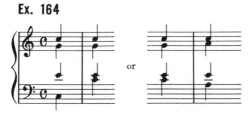

In any event free choice is possible in the harmonization of an anacrusis.

The inner voices

The completion of our harmonization awaits only the filling in of the inner voices. Here no particular problem that has not been previously discussed will arise. Some of the resultant harmonizations appear below. All are grammatically correct. Some will prefer one setting to the others. This is a matter of taste and cannot be debated.

Ex. 165

In all types of exercises, melodic and harmonic patterns will be found at times. These consist of a short initial succession (figure) in either or both of the outer voices that is repeated exactly with an upward or downward transposition (sequence). The remaining voices should always transpose as exactly as possible the progressions that they are given in the figure. In Example 121*a*, the first two chords form a figure that is repeated sequentially three times. Observe the sequential construction of all voices. The only departure from a strict adherence to the figure occurs in the tenor in the sixth chord where D is written instead of B to avoid a doubled seventh step. The same remarks apply to Example 121*b*. Short sequences will be found in Examples 138*b*, *c*, *d*, and 139.

Choral and keyboard style compared

Assignments will be made for keyboard performance in a simple and easily playable style. The essential differences between choral and keyboard style are determined by the limited span of the hands and the manner of performance adopted here. Three voices will be played by the right hand and one, the bass, by the left. In notating for this manner of performance the three upper parts should be grouped together, usually in the G clef. The bass part, played by the left hand, should be placed in the bass clef. The total range should be limited to the four middle octaves of the keyboard, the equivalent of the total range from the bass voice to the soprano in choral style. For purposes of clarification, Example 166*a* is a choral notation of the keyboard excerpt of Example 166 *b*. In this transcription the only modification is the manner of notation.

The transcription in Example 166*c* from a choral to a keyboard style includes modifications of voice leading to fit the prescribed manner of keyboard performance. Compare this with Example 165*a*, particularly the differences at the turn of bar 2. The leaps in the right hand, following the cadence on the C chord, are necessary for convenience of keyboard performance, but would be difficult for voices. The similar leaps of Example 165*b* are caused solely by difficulties of voice leading. Note that this kind of adjustment is most conveniently made after a cadence.

Ex. 166[7]

a.

b.

c.

Notation

Observe in Example 166*b* that the three upper parts of chords are joined by a common stem. There is a pitch area around the B above middle C where stems may point upward or downward, depending on the spacing of the tones of each chord and on the stems of surrounding chords. Note that an upward stemming is retained through bar 2 of Example 166*b*, even though the top note reaches D. Generally, chords with top notes lying on B or higher are notated with stems pointing downward, and upward when the top note lies on A or below. If the range of all parts is low, all parts may be notated in the bass clef, as in Example 167, bar 1.

---

[7] Ex. 166*b*. Chopin, Nocturne, Op. 15, No. 3, bars 89–92.

Ex. 167 [8]

Independent rhythms in one of the parts are notated with separate stems. In Example 168, compare the notation of bar 1 with bar 2. The aim should be a clear indication of the motion of each part.

Ex. 168

As a rule, bass notes from the middle line of the bass clef upward bear downward stems. Below the middle line, D, they are stemmed upward, as in the preceding examples. Occasionally a beam joining a group of notes, as in bar 2 of Example 168, must adjust itself to the range of the entire passage.

Brief illustrations of keyboard notation will be found in Examples 268*b*, 322, 325, 358*d*, *e*, and 362*c*, *d*, and *e*. The style and notation used in our work approximate eighteenth-century figured bass accompaniments.

THREE PART EXERCISES

Exercises in three parts introduce a lighter texture and permit greater independence and agility in part writing. Many more incomplete chords appear, represented only by the root and third or, at cadences, by the tripled root. The thinner texture of three part writing makes it easier to introduce the VII, partly because the bothersome problem of doubling does not arise in normal use.

Example 169 contains several noteworthy features of three part construction and notation. The first part of each illustration is written in vocal nota-

[8] Chopin, Nocturne, Op. 37, No. 1, middle section.

tion, the second part in keyboard notation. Example 169*a* shows a normal complete triad; no tones are doubled. The usual and preferred incomplete chord appears in Example 169*b*; note the doubling of the root and the omission of the fifth. The incomplete chord of Example 169*c* with the third omitted is less frequent and in most cases to be avoided in the company of such chords as appear in 169*a* and *b*. A frequent form of complete cadence is shown in Example 169*d*. Note the final chord with a tripled root, brought about by the melodic action of the leading tone. Such a setting is preferable to Example 169*e* with its needlessly large leap. A brief example of three part writing appears in Example 169*f*. Observe the doubling and the total of only five complete triads out of the nine chords used.

Ex. 169

10

Position
of the
Sixth

Definition

A triad is in the position of the sixth, or the six-three position, when the bass forms a sixth and a third with the tones above, as shown earlier in Example 90*b* and *e*. Such a construction may be the first inversion of the chord whose root lies a third below the bass tone (Example 170*a*). Or it may represent solely the bass note upon which it is built (Example 170*b*). A basis for distinguishing between the two origins will be presented in this chapter.

Figured bass signatures

The figured bass indication is $^6_3$ or simply 6, regardless of the derivation of the position. On occasion, as we shall see under *Doubling,* and in Example 170*c, d, e,* one or another of the figures may be duplicated to form six-six-three or six-three-three. The position may also be indicated by the signature, eight-six-three.

Doubling

Doubling procedures are the same as for the five-three or root position,[1] but may be conveniently restated in terms of the interval content of the new position. As indicated in Example 170c, the best tones to double are the sixth and the third above the bass. Example 170d with the doubled bass note (eight-six-three) is less frequent than the others. Remember to avoid the doubled leading tone (six-three-three in the V6 and six-six-three in the VII6) as in Example 170e.

Ex. 170

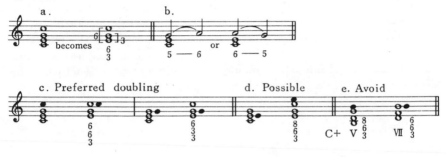

Diminished triads in the position of the sixth

The success of many of the new possibilities of voice leading to be discussed in this chapter is dependent on the fact that diminished triads have a much more favorable arrangement of intervals in the position of the sixth than in root position. The stigma attached to the diminished fifth when it appears as a chord-defining interval between the bass and one of the upper voices is reduced to a minimum in the position of the sixth because it is covered by the new defining intervals of a sixth and a third.

Ex. 171

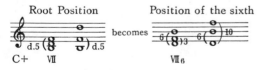

[1] Review Ch. 6, *Doubling*.

Thus the diminished triad in this position is defined by the same intervals as those that comprise major and minor triads.

Ex. 172

Because the deficient diminished fifth or its inversion, the augmented fourth, plays a subsidiary role when the triad is expressed in this position, it is relieved of the prescriptions that limit its use in root position.

Because our attention thus far has been centered on the major mode, we have been confronted by only one diminished triad, the VII. There are two more with which we shall have to deal when a study is made of the minor mode. The II in the pure minor mode is diminished, as is VI when the sixth step of the scale is raised (Example 173).

Ex. 173

All diminished triads are much more certain of success in the position of the sixth than in root position.

ALTERNATE EXECUTION OF EARLIER TECHNIQUES

Certain techniques originally discussed during the study of root position appear in alternate forms when the position of the sixth is introduced.

1. Successive skips in the bass in the natural succession[2] are greatly reduced when alternate chords are constructed in the position of the sixth.

---

[2] Compare Ex. 174 and 121.

Ex. 174

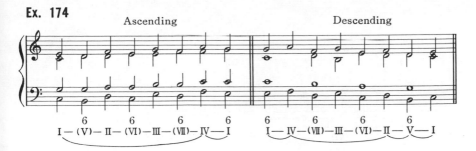

It follows that the natural relationship of chords whose roots lie a fifth apart may be realized without the necessity of leaping a fifth in the bass.[3]

Ex. 175

2. Certain chords that were originally inserted in root position to avoid faulty voice leading may be expressed in the position of the sixth and accomplish the same end:[4]

Ex. 176

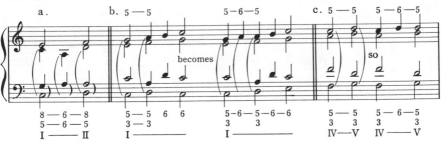

[3] Compare Ex. 175 and 125.
[4] Compare Ex. 176a and 138b; 176c and 138a; 177 and 139a.

Ex. 177

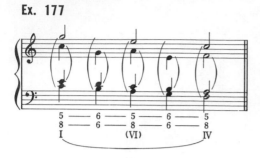

NEW TECHNIQUES

To these last two examples the following may be added wherein passing chords that are impossible when triads are limited to root position become free of fault when the position of the sixth is used:[5]

Ex. 178

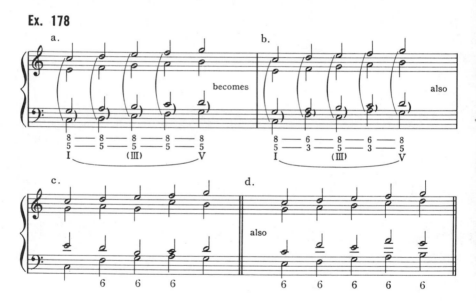

Parallel motion

For many centuries, the position of the sixth has been regarded as the ideal sonority for passages moving in parallel motion. For such purposes, three part constructions, as in Example 179a, are easier to handle

[5] Compare Ex. 178b and 138b.

than four part constructions (Example 178*c, d*) with their problems of doubling. Note, however, that the danger of parallel fifths is realized, as in Example 179*b*, when the third of the six-three lies above the sixth. This caution applies to four as well as three part writing. A technique for the averting of such a hazard appears in Example 179*c*.

Ex. 179

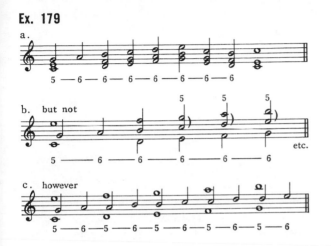

Neighboring chords

In the following examples the characteristic motion that creates the intermediate chords is that of a neighboring tone in either the bass or the upper voice. This motion rather than the vertical identity of each dependent chord accounts for its function.

Ex. 180

Inversions

One of the most important features of the position of the sixth is that it permits the bass to express two tones of the same chord, the root and the third. It is in this use that the six-three represents most clearly an inversion of the chord whose root lies a third below the bass tone.

Ex. 181

This double representation of one harmony makes for much more elasticity in connections, for the bass can set as its temporary plan the connecting of the two positions either directly as in Example 181 or indirectly by making use of intermediate passing or neighboring tones and their triads. Study the motion of the bass in Example 182.

Ex. 182

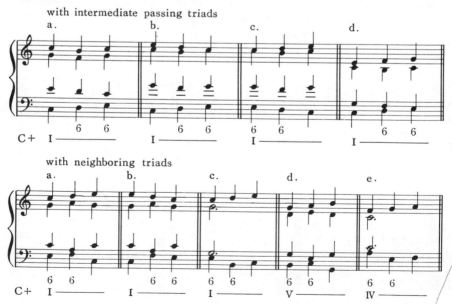

When this third in the bass is inverted to a sixth, an intermediate chord is often inserted to break up the leap (Example 183).

Ex. 183

A comparison of the sopranos and basses of Examples 182 and 183 will illustrate a few of the alternate ways in which to harmonize the same pattern of notes.

For example, the two harmonizations below accomplish the same purpose. Selection of one over the other is a matter of free choice (Example 184).

Ex. 184

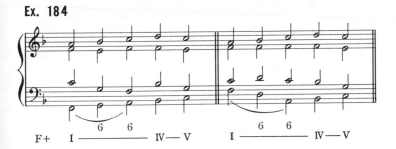

Association of VII₆ and V

In Chapter 8 it was established that VII is associated with V because of the tones common to both triads.[6] This association is much stronger than any other in the major mode because both triads move readily to I: V because its root lies a fifth above the root of I, and VII because its diminished fifth resolves to tones that suggest I. This relationship operates in many ways:

1. The fourth step of the scale may be given a dominant harmonization by using VII or VII₆ (Example 185).

[6] Review Ex. 128.

Ex. 185

2. VII$_6$ may be employed as a substitute for V in those cases in which the use of V produces parallel fifths (Example 186).

Ex. 186

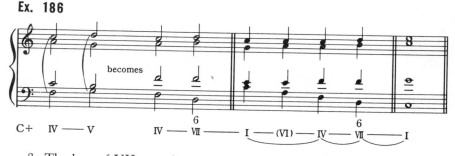

3. The bass of VII$_6$ may be regarded as a temporary goal of motion from the bass of V, in the same sense that a root and its third may set the plan of a connection (Example 187).

Ex. 187

POSITION OF THE SIXTH IN CADENCES

In complete cadences the formal demand for harmonic clarity is best satisfied by retaining the characteristic leap of a fifth in the bass from the root of V, the penultimate chord, to the root of I. The chord antecedent to

V, the antepenultimate chord, may be used either in root position or in the position of the sixth. This increases the harmonic possibilities of the cadential bass (Example 188).

Ex. 188

The one exception to this demand for expression of the cadential V-I in root position is at less important melodic halts that come at the end of rhythmic groups or short phrases where V_6 (or VII_6) -I may be used, as in the first melodic halt in Example 189a. The four bars make one phrase with a subdivision in the second bar. Compare the complete cadential bass in Example 189a with the basses in Examples b and c.

Ex. 189

Similarly in the complete plagal cadence IV-I both triads should be in root position. Occasionally a melodic variant produces II_6 rather than IV. The characteristic bass, however, reveals the essential plagal nature of the cadence (Example 190).

Ex. 190

Ex. 191

In incomplete cadences the final chord is most stable and hence most cadential when placed in root position. The antecedent chords may be expressed in either root position or the position of the sixth (Example 191).

The aim of the deceptive cadence is best satisfied when the last two chords, V-VI, are kept in root position (Example 192).

Ex. 192

Role of the Middle Voices

In harmonizing melodies, the middle voices assume a new importance because the tones given to them very often make the difference between root position and the position of the sixth. When a triad is expressed in root position, the intervals it may form with the three upper voices are an octave, a fifth, and a third (Example 193).

Ex. 193

In the position of the sixth, the bass may form the intervals of an octave, a sixth, and a third with the upper voices (Example 194).

Ex. 194

Thus two intervals, the octave and the third, are common to both positions. When either of these intervals appears in the outer voices, it is up to the middle voices to identify the triad and its position (Example 195).

Ex. 195

It is important to try out both possibilities whenever doubt exists. For example, in the passing chord between I and I_6 in Example 196 the alto makes the difference between a VII_6 and a II.

Ex. 196

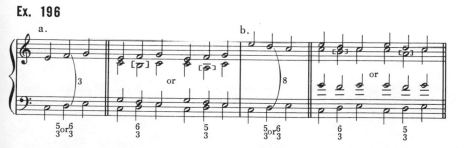

Of course, when the outer voices stand a fifth apart, only root position is possible. Similarly when they are a sixth apart, only the position of the sixth, for the time being, can be expressed. The middle voices in these two cases merely fill in the chord and play no role in identifying the triad and its position (Example 197).

Ex. 197

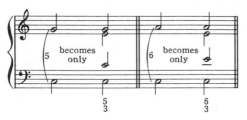

Thus, $\frac{6}{3}$ and $\frac{5}{3}$ are related in two ways. The first is a chordal relationship in which the root or the third of the same chord may appear in the bass, as in Example 198.

Ex. 198

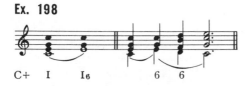

The second is a voice-leading relationship in which any bass tone may be made into $\frac{5}{3}$ or $\frac{6}{3}$ by the upper parts (Example 199).

Ex. 199

Both ways of generating the position of the sixth have important uses and should be remembered.

FAULTY WEAK-STRONG REPETITIONS IN THE BASS

Mixtures of root position and the position of the sixth present more insidious temptations to repeat tones awkwardly in the bass from a weak to a strong beat.[7] These repetitions should be avoided in the interests of a clear statement of the meter. On the other hand strong-weak, strong-strong, and strong-weak-strong repetitions are metrically good.

Ex. 200

SUMMARY

1. Chords and techniques.
   a. Diminished triads may be expressed without restriction in the $\frac{6}{3}$ position (Examples 171–173).
   b. The natural successions, ascending and descending, may be expressed with alternate chords in the position of the sixth (Examples 174, 175).
   c. Chords in the position of the sixth may be used as alternatives to root position in detail work, such as the correction of faulty voice leading and the harmonization of dependent tones (Examples 176, 177, 180, 196).
   d. New techniques of detail are made available through use of the position of the sixth (Examples 178, 179, 182, 185–187).
2. The bass.
   a. The position of the sixth helps to reduce the number of leaps in the bass and the angularity of basses made up of root position alone. Compare all examples in this chapter with those in Chapter 8.
   b. Either the root or the third of a chord may now be assigned to the bass (Examples 181–184).
   c. Increased caution is necessary to avoid the many new possibilities of expressing weak-strong repetitions in the bass (Example 200).
3. The inner voices.
   a. The inner voices determine the position of a chord when the outer voices are an octave or a third apart (Examples 193–196).
   b. The inner voices merely complete the chord when the outer voices are a fifth or sixth apart (Example 197).
4. Cadences.
   a. Use of the position of the sixth in complete cadences is restricted to the antepenultimate chord (Examples 188 and 190)); in incomplete

---

[7] Review Ch. 9, *The metric nature of the bass.*

cadences it is restricted to the penultimate. In lesser melodic halts it may be used without restrictions of a formal nature (Example 189).

5. Chord meaning. Five-three and six-three are related in two ways:

    a. As root position and first inversion (Examples 170a, 181–184, 198). Here, two bass notes lying a third apart represent the same harmony, as in I, I$_5$.

    b. As a voice leading relationship (Examples 170b, 176b, c, 190, 199). Here, five-three and six-three share the same bass note, as in I$_{5-6}$.

11

The Minor Mode

Contrast Between Major and Minor

The musical value of the minor mode is that it acts as a contrast to the major mode built from the same tonic degree. This is most evident when comparison is made of the qualities of triads in the pure minor with those of the major mode. The three primary triads, I, IV, and V, are major in quality in the major mode[1] and minor in quality in the minor mode, a relationship that obtains between no other mode and major.

Ex. 201

Qualities of triads in the pure minor mode

1. Minor triads	I , IV, V	
2. Major triads	III , VI , VII	
3. Diminished triad	II	

[1] Compare Ex. 201 and 89.

113

Location of the diminished fifth

Until the present time our attention has been focused on the major mode because, in its original form, the major mode embraces and utilizes the natural fifth and compromises with it (between the seventh and fourth steps) in a particularly felicitous way. At no time do chromatic alterations have to be imposed as correctives. The minor scale in its pure, original form is not capable of such unambiguous expression. Certain correctives are necessary and these cause difficulty in employing it successfully.

This ambiguity has two causes. The first involves the position, between the second and sixth steps, of the diminished fifth.

Ex. 202

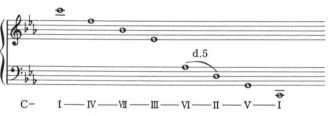

This diminished fifth, because it resolves normally to tones that suggest a triad different from the tonic, has a way of emphasizing as the center of activity the III rather than the I.[2]

Ex. 203

The second cause of ambiguity is the listless melodic relationship between the seventh and eighth steps of the mode as compared with the active relationship between the seventh and eighth steps in the major mode.

[2] Review in Ch. 2, *Melodically active half step relationship* and *The leading tone.*

Ex. 204

Treatment of the seventh step

In order to combat the ambiguity of the minor mode, the raised seventh step or leading tone is often borrowed from the major mode and used instead of the original seventh step. It is this borrowing or interchanging of steps from one mode to another that gives rise to the mixed scales that were discussed earlier.[3] Three general situations arise in which the seventh step (or subtonic) appears. The student must learn to distinguish one from the others in order to use the desired form of the step, raised or original. They are:

(1) Progressions that require the leading tone.
(2) Progressions in which either form of seventh step may be used.
(3) Progressions that require the original seventh step.

1. Progressions that require the leading tone. Whenever it is necessary to point out the location of the key center, the leading tone is used. This occurs in the succession V-I or VII-I in all positions, in incomplete cadences ending on V or VII, and in the deceptive cadence V-VI.

Employment of the leading tone when the dominant or its associate, VII, moves to I, affirms the tonic chord as the center of orientation, as in Example 205.[4]

Ex. 205

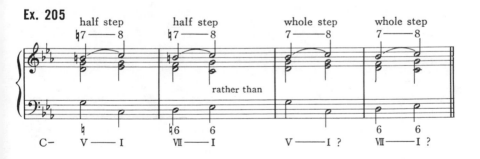

---

[3] Review in Ch. 2, *Mixed Scales.*
[4] For the meaning of accidentals in figured basses see the following section, *Chromatic Figured Bass Signatures.*

In incomplete cadences that end on V or VII, the leading tone adds to the tonic expectancy of the dominant and thus clarifies its harmonic status. In the deceptive cadence V-VI, the leading tone is required in order to make the deception persuasive. Observe that this rule applies only to the *cadential* V-VI.

Ex. 206

2. *Progressions in which either form of the seventh step may be used.* Most of the progressions not included in the cases mentioned above may be treated optionally. They include the V or VII chords when, aside from incomplete cadences, they are not succeeded by I, and many progressions in which III appears. Here it is instructive to try both the leading tone and the seventh step in order to test their differences in effect as in Example 207.

Ex. 207

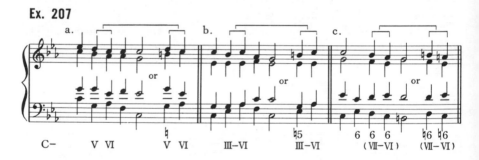

3. *Progressions that require the original seventh step.* Many progressions will be met in which use of the leading tone brings about an involved melodic relationship, the augmented second, or an involved chromatic interchange, the cross relation, both of which will be discussed in the following sections. Unless the voice leading can be modified to eliminate both of these relatively complex relationships, it is simpler and therefore advisable to use the original seventh step.

Ex. 208

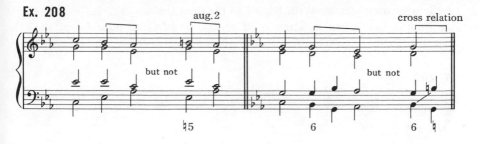

Conclusion. Observe that each of the three cases is concerned with a progression rather than an isolated chord. Thus the leading tone or the seventh step is employed according to the context in which it occurs, rather than the chord with which it happens to be identified. Further, the progressions described under *1,* those which *require* a leading tone, are the most critical for they are concerned with a constructive function rather than an option. Each progression should first be analyzed to determine whether it belongs to this case. If it does not, test it against the characteristic features of the two remaining cases.

CHROMATIC FIGURED BASS SIGNATURES

Chromatic alterations of the seventh and sixth steps, and all other chromatic changes, are indicated in figured bass signatures by appropriate accidentals placed to the left of the affected figure. Thus, ♮6,♯ ♭6, 6 mean that the written sixth above the bass should be preceded by the accidental indicated, as in Example 207*c.* An accidental without a following figure, as in Example 206, bar 2, always refers to the third above the bass. When the written bass note bears an accidental, the tones of unaltered figures agree with the prevailing key signature, as in Example 206, bar 1. If the figured bass signature, as well as the written bass note, is altered chromatically, the written notes should be altered accordingly, as in Examples 418*b,* bar 7, and 419*a,* bar 2.

CHROMATIC PROGRESSIONS

The augmented second

Use of the leading tone presents two new problems of voice leading: the augmented second and the cross relation, both of which were mentioned in the preceding section. With regard to the first, the use in a single voice of the leading tone when it is preceded or followed by the pure minor sixth step introduces a complex mixed interval, the augmented second.

Ex. 209

As at the beginning of the study of elementary harmony preference is always given to the simple over the complex, the melodic progression of an augmented second is not to be used, but is to be replaced by the simpler melodic progressions of a major and minor second and a minor third. To avoid a threatening augmented second, there are two methods, each of which has two subdivisions:

1*a*. Approach the leading tone from above:

Ex. 210

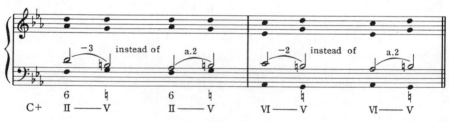

b. Quit the leading tone by upward motion:

Ex. 211

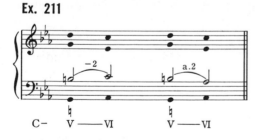

2*a*. Raise the sixth step when it moves to the raised seventh step:

Ex. 212

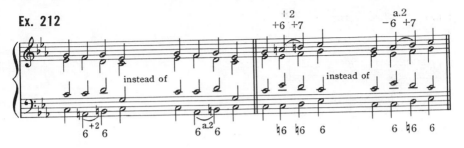

b. Raise the sixth step when it is preceded by the raised seventh step:

Ex. 213

The augmented second is classified with difficult melodic leaps such as the augmented fourth, the diminished fifth, and major and minor sevenths, which should give way to simpler melodic motions in the early stages of the study of voice leading.[5] It should not be confused with the like-sounding minor third. The minor third is a diatonic interval and occurs in relatively simple situations while the augmented second is, as we have seen, a complex mixed interval occurring in only one contrived situation.

The cross relation

Along with the augmented second, the variability of the sixth and seventh steps gives rise to the threat of a cross relation, that is, the appearance of a tone in one voice followed by a chromatic alteration of the same tone in another voice.

5 Review in Ch. 7, *Conjunct and disjunct motion.*

Ex. 214

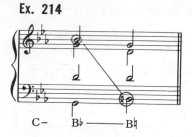

Not all cross relations are bad, but the testing of them belongs properly to
that later stage of our work at which involved relationships will be studied.[6]
Our concern here is with the origins of relationships and their simplest
applications. The chromatically altered tone has its origin as a substitute for
an indigenous note and arises, in those cases with which we are concerned,
out of a partial motion away from or a partial motion toward the original
note.

Ex. 215

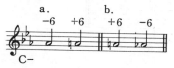

The complete motion in its simplest execution belongs properly in one voice.
To avoid a cross relation, keep in a single voice chromatic progressions
involving two forms of the same tone.

Ex. 216

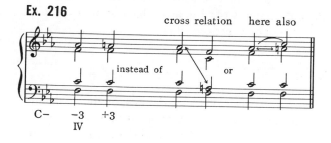

---

[6] Specifically, in Ch. 17.

DIMINISHED TRIADS IN MINOR

The minor mode presents three possible diminished triads:

A. The II in pure minor:

Ex. 217

B. The VII when the seventh step is raised:

Ex. 218

C. The VI when the sixth step is raised:

Ex. 219

The precautions that must be taken when these triads are expressed in root position and the consequent advisability of limiting their use to the position of the sixth have already been discussed.[7]

---

[7] Review in Ch. 8, *The VII,* and in Ch. 10, *Diminished triads in the position of the sixth.*

SUMMARY

The use of the minor mode involves the following recommendations and prohibitions:

A. Recommendations.

    1*a*. Use the leading tone in the progressions

$$\left.\begin{array}{l} V \\ V_6 \\ VII \\ VII_6 \end{array}\right\} \; I \;(\text{or } I_6)$$

    b. Use the leading tone in the V or VII in incomplete cadences, and in the deceptive cadence V-VI.

    2.   When the seventh step is present in progressions or circumstances other than those above, follow the recommendations of Examples 207 and 208.

B. Prohibitions.

    1.   Avoid the melodic relationship of an augmented second (pure minor sixth step to raised seventh or raised seventh to pure minor sixth).

    2.   Avoid the cross relation.

    3.   Avoid awkward uses of diminished triads, now increased in number (Examples 217–219).

CONCLUSION

For the rest, all of the relationships that have been employed in the major mode, such as the natural succession of triads, the association of triads whose roots lie a third apart, and the various voice-leading origins of chords, apply equally well to the minor mode.

12

The Six-Four Position

The six-four position occurs when the lowest note of a triad forms a sixth and a fourth with the tones that lie above, as indicated earlier in Example 90 *c* and *f*. Such a position may be the second inversion of the chord whose root lies a fifth below the bass note. Or it may represent a combination of tones engaged in a voice leading or horizontal task. The *figured bass signature* is most usually $^6_4$, as indicated in Example 220a. It can be amplified by a duplication of either of the figures (thus, six-six-four, or six-four-four). At times, it is represented as eight-six-four. In *doubling,* it is customary to duplicate the bass note, as indicated in Example 220b.

Ex. 220

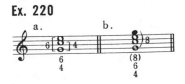

THE INCONCLUSIVE NATURE OF SIX-FOUR

Of the three positions in which a triad may be expressed, the $^6_4$ is the most difficult to use successfully. The reason for this is that two secondary consonances, the sixth and the fourth, make up the defining intervals between the bass and the upper voices. It was pointed out in discussing the nature of consonance that these two intervals are completely stable or consonant only in the confirming presence of the parent fundamental tone.[1] The only opportunity that this fundamental tone or root has to vouch for the stability of the secondary consonances, when the $\frac{6}{4}$ position is expressed, is to appear prominently in the bass of preceding or following chords. The $\frac{4}{6}$ by itself is powerless to provide conclusive information about its nature. Context alone will define its character. The context can do either of two things: it may fail to present the original root, in which case the $\frac{6}{4}$ becomes highly unstable and dependent; or it may present the root, in which case the essential consonance and stability of the position will be established. Our description of the characteristic uses of the $\frac{6}{4}$ will be divided to conform with the two kinds of context. The first section of the following discussion will describe the unstable or active $\frac{6}{4}$; the second section, the stable $\frac{6}{4}$.

THE UNSTABLE SIX-FOUR

6-5
4-3

The most frequent use of the $\frac{6}{4}$ as an active position is that in which its lowest tone remains stationary to become the root of the following chord: As the bass in such a connection is either a held or a repeated tone, it normally commences on a strong pulse.[2] For this reason, the $\frac{6}{4}$ in this use is called the accented $\frac{6}{4}$.

Ex. 221

metric scheme

The tones that make up such a $\frac{6}{4}$ are so completely dependent on their surrounding stronger chords that they create the impression of a fortuitous combination engaged in a horizontal mission. The fact that the tones add up to a chord with a harmonic root is purely incidental to this function. Thus although in Example 222*b* it is *literally* correct to label the progression IV-I$\frac{6}{4}$-V, it is truer to the *spirit* of the connection to distinguish between the harmonically strong and definite IV and V and the incidental $\frac{6}{4}$ by label-

---

[1] Review in Ch. 4, *Secondary consonances.*
[2] Review in Ch. 9, *The metric nature of the bass.*

ing the progression IV-V $^{6-5}_{4-3}$. In doing this, acknowledgment is paid to the impression that the $^6_4$ represents nothing more than a delay in the arrival of the tones that really matter harmonically. In Examples 222*g* and *h*, decorations in the middle voices form the $^6_4$.

Ex. 222

$^{6-5}_{4-3}$ *in harmonizing melodies*

In the melodic fragments of Example 223, the success of the $^6_4$ is determined solely by the metric position of the passing tone E.

Ex. 223

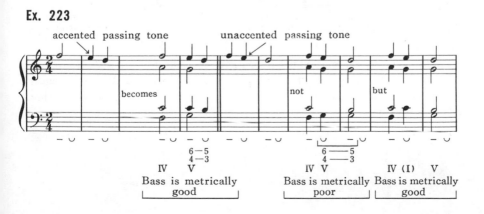

Considered from the point of view of the harmonization of melodies, the formula $^{6-5}_{4-3}$ may be applied only to descending accented passing or neighboring tones. Its most frequent use is at cadences where V, according to the condition of the upper voices, may be expressed simply or in terms of $^{6-5}_{4-3}$. This applies to all dominant cadences, whether complete or incomplete. The most usual dominant cadences may be summarized as follows:

$$
\left.
\begin{array}{l}
\left.
\begin{array}{l}
\text{II} \\
\text{IV} \\
\text{or} \\
\text{II}_6
\end{array}
\right\} \\
\left.
\begin{array}{l}
\text{IV}_6 \\
\text{or} \\
\text{IV}
\end{array}
\right\}
\end{array}
\right\}
\quad
\left\{
\begin{array}{l}
\text{V} \\
\text{or} \\
\text{6--5} \\
\text{4--3} \\
\text{V}
\end{array}
\right\}
-
\left\{
\begin{array}{l}
\text{I} \\
\text{or} \\
\text{VI}
\end{array}
\right.
$$

An examination of the doubling in the $^6_4$ of Examples 222 and 223 will reveal that it is most convenient to double the bass, as that tone becomes the root when $^6_4$ resolves to $^5_3$.

The formula $^{6-5}_{4-3}$ is usually, but by no means exclusively, built on the tonic (I^{6-5}_{4-3}) and the dominant (V^{6-5}_{4-3}) steps of the scale.

5-6
3-4

Rhythmically, the accented neighbor or passing tone shares that part of the beat or measure which belongs in conception to the following principal tone, and therefore owes its existence more to the succeeding than to the preceding principal tone. The opposite is true of the unaccented passing or neighboring tone; it is more dependent on the preceding principal tone whose beat it shares.

Ex. 224

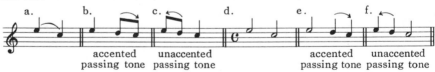

Thus we relate the accented dependent $^6_4$ to the following $^5_3$. Conversely, the unaccented $^6_4$ is related to the preceding accented $^5_3$. All the accentual conditions that characterize the formula $^{5-6}_{3-4}$ are the exact opposites of those that govern $^{6-5}_{4-3}$.

Ex. 225

$^{5-6}_{3-4}$ may be applied to an unaccented neighbor or passing tone.

Study of Example 226 will reveal that:

Ex. 226

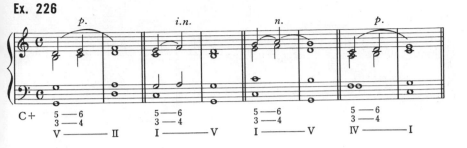

1. The bass of the $^5_3$ remains stationary.
2. The bass of the $^6_4$ is the most convenient tone to double.
3. The horizontal function of the $^6_4$ depends on the nature of the upper voices.

5-6-5
3-4-3

Both of the preceding formulae are occasionally combined to form a neighboring $^6_4$. The metric position of the $^6_4$ is variable. Observe the stationary bass in Example 227.

Ex. 227

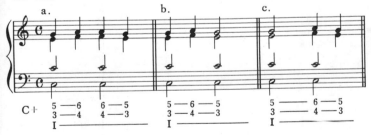

Six-four formed by a passing bass

In the preceding description of the dependent $^6_4$ it has been characterized as passing or neighboring according to the precise nature of the motion of the upper voices. The bass, in passing through the interval of a third, sometimes forms a $^6_4$ with the upper voices. This particular use of the

$^6_4$ is described as a passing $^6_4$ because of the determinative form of the bass.[3] The upper voices are variable, as is the metric position (Example 228).

Ex. 228

THE STABLE SIX-FOUR

The stability of the sixth and fourth that form the defining intervals of the $^6_4$ can be asserted most easily through the contextual presence of stronger, more determinate positions of the same chord. The variable secondary consonances are then provided with the necessary support provided by primary consonances. In its simplest form the bass reaches the $^6_4$ through an arpeggio from root position in one and the same chord.

Ex. 229

In the preceding examples the $^6_4$ is so completely covered by the stronger root position that its intervals are accepted as consonant. This contextual proof of the consonance and hence the stability of the $^6_4$ may be applied in an endless variety of ways. The root need not appear below the bass of the $^6_4$. Whether above or below in the bass of the surrounding chords, its definitive presence will stabilize the $^6_4$. This is most apparent in the simplest kind of waltz or march accompaniment where a threatening drone in the bass is avoided by the use of an alternate to the root.

---

[3] Compare Ex. 228 and 182*a* to *d*.

Ex. 230

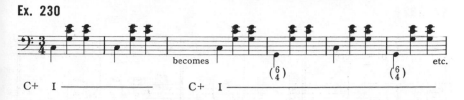

C+ I ———————   C+ I ——————————

Thus Beethoven writes in the opening bars of the last movement of opus 18, No. 6. Even the rhythmically accented F in bar 1 cannot disprove the governing nature of the root B–flat. The construction of this bar influences that of the second bar which stands, in terms of voice leading, for V_6 and not V, with the E–flat in the middle voice as a chord seventh. Note the interesting variant in bar 3 of the downward leap of the bass. Instead of a leap from A to F, the passing tone, G, is inserted.

Ex. 231

The $^6_4$ is much more dubious when the root follows rather than precedes it. Brahms's use of this technique was particularly masterful. Until the root arrives in the following quotation from "Botschaft," we do not know conclusively whether the $^6_4$ is stable or unstable. Example 232*a* is a reduction of the two bars. In Examples *b, c,* and *d* the remaining decorative tones are inserted.

Ex. 232

As Example 232*a* reveals, this is an application of the stable $^6_4$ as a detail of an arpeggio bass.

MIDDLE VOICES AND THE SIX-FOUR

In the harmonization of melodies, certain outer voice intervals offer no conclusive information concerning the identity and position of the chord used. Therefore it is up to the middle voices to form the characteristic intervals with the bass that will crystallize the chord. A comparison of the interval content of each position built from the same bass tone will reveal the common intervals.

Ex. 233

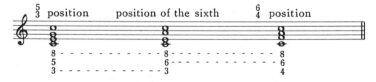

An octave between outer voices may be filled in to stand for any one of the three possible positions.

Ex. 234

A sixth between outer voices may be filled in to stand for either the $\frac{6}{4}$ position or the position of the sixth.

Ex. 235

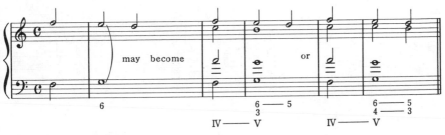

A third (or tenth) between outer voices may be filled in to stand for either five-three position or the position of the sixth. This has already been illustrated.[4]

Outer voices define the chord only when they stand a fifth apart, in which case only five-three position may be expressed, and when they stand a fourth apart, in which case only the six-four position may be expressed (Example 236).

Ex. 236

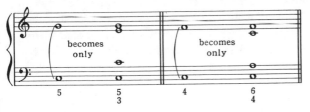

[4] Review in Ch. 10, *Role of the Middle Voices.*

The differences between the stable and the unstable $^6_4$ are these:

1. The unstable $^6_4$ is built on either a stationary or a stepwise bass. There may be a leap to the stationary bass when $^{6-5}_{4-3}$ is used (Example 222*h*); there may be a leap away from the stationary bass when $^{5-6}_{3-4}$ is used (Example 226).

2. There may be a leap both to and from the bass of the stable $^6_4$, but at least one of those leaps is to or from a stronger position of the chord whose tones form the $^6_4$ (Example 229).

Example 237 summarizes in brief the various $^6_4$ techniques. Study the behavior of the bass and the doubling.

Ex. 237

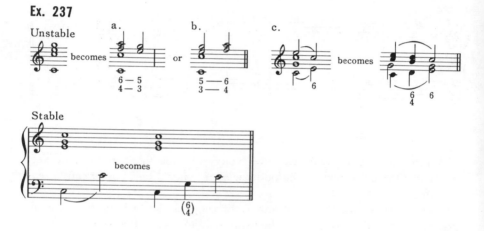

These are the characteristic uses of the $^6_4$ position. Because it is so indeterminate by itself, it depends entirely on its context for a definition of its meaning. There is no other chord position that can be so easily maltreated. That we may learn to appreciate the double life that the $^6_4$ leads, it has been described in its most elementary uses. Nevertheless in its expanded uses in free composition it still must look to its context for clarification of its use as stable, representing its own root position in the form of a second inversion, or as unstable, representing a horizontally conceived combination of tones.

13

Tones of Figuration, Melodic

We have seen that in most situations the $^6_4$ position arises so completely out of the horizontal motion of voices that it becomes nothing more than a vertical accident. As such, it tends to lose its harmonic significance and to acquire meaning only through its horizontal context, through the way in which the tones that form it act as dependent passing or neighboring tones. The unstable $^6_4$ thus seems to be an ambiguous arrangement of tones, for as we *see* it, it appears to be capable of vertical explanation: that is, it can be "uninverted" and traced back to an original root position. But as we *hear* it, it represents so completely a detail of movement that to attribute harmonic meaning to it belies its real function. In this chapter a further study will be made of tones that arise as incidents of melodic motion or figuration. In Chapter 14 figurational tones of rhythmic origin will be discussed.

The Chordal Skip

Description

The chordal skip (c.s.) may be used as a means of partially filling in a leap.

Ex. 238

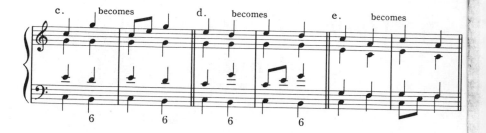

It may also be used to establish or continue an eighth-note motion.

Ex. 239

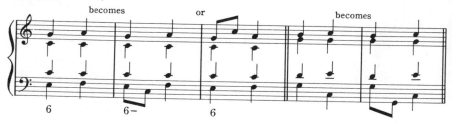

It should be noted that throughout Examples 238 and 239 the skip is to a tone in the *prevailing* chord, not to one in the approaching chord.

Ex. 240

Skip in prevailing
chord

Skip in approaching
chord

Faulty parallel motions caused by chordal skips

Care must be exercised to avoid chordal skips that create faulty parallel motion in the unison, fifth, or octave.

Ex. 241

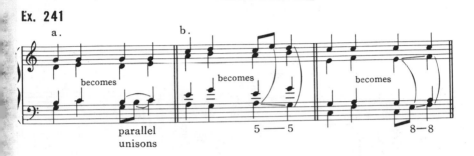

The tone to which the skip is made, although a detail of decoration, is a chord tone and as such retains its vertical meaning for voice leading.

Faulty parallel motions corrected by chordal skips

Because the chordal skip is of vertical consequence, it may be used to break up a direct succession of octaves, fifths, or unisons,[1] as in Example 242.

Ex. 242[2]

[1] For a more extended discussion of parallel fifths as well as for more examples in instrumental and vocal music, consult Johannes Brahms, *Oktaven u. Quinten u. A.*, ed. Heinrich Schenker, Universal edition 10,508 Wien.

[2] Ex. *a,* "Jesu, der du selbst so wohl," bar 15.

Ex. *b,* "In dich hab' ich gehoffet, Herr," bar 7.

Ex. *c,* "Christus, der uns selig macht," bar 7.

Ex. *d,* "Herzlich thut mich verlangen," bar 2.

Ex. *e,* "Gelobet seist du, Jesu Christ," bar 1.

Ex. *f,* "Unter deinen Schirmen," bar 1.

Ex. *g,* "Die Sonn' hat," bar 8.

Ex. 242 (cont'd)

THE PASSING TONE

Description

As a detail of melodic figuration, the vertical significance of the passing tone (p.) is dwarfed by the fact that it does not receive the endorsement of an independent bass tone and chord. It is in this respect that it is different from the passing tones that have in one way or another been harmonized and have thus assumed a more important function in carrying out the underlying plan of a melody. The passing tone fits most happily in the interval of a third.

Ex. 243

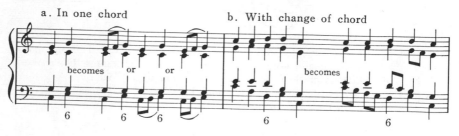

In Examples 242 and 243 the passing tone falls on the weak part of a divided beat. The introduction of a passing tone on the heavy part of a divided beat brings it into higher relief and delays the entrance of the chord tone toward which it is moving. The result is that the tones that belong together vertically are not sounded together. Note the parallel fifths in Example 244*a*. They will be discussed in the following section.

Ex. 244

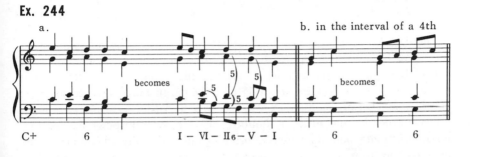

Parallel fifths caused and corrected by passing tones

Passing tones (and also neighboring tones), in the sense in which they are being discussed in this chapter, are interpolated tones. The intervals that they form with other voices are of an incidental and accidental nature. The real intervals are those created by chord tones. Until the present time our attention has been directed solely to the manipulation of these chord tones, in other words, to the manipulation of real intervals. For this reason parallel fifths, a relationship thwarting independence of voice motion, have been avoided. With the introduction of incidental tones, the problem assumes a new aspect, which may be viewed from two angles:

1. If the real, chordal intervals are good, the interpolated interval caused by a tone of figuration is insignificant.

2. If the real, chordal intervals are in faulty relationship, the interpolated interval may, under certain conditions, correct the fault.

The important, active factor in the first case is harmonic expectancy. Our ears hear through the incidental relationships and assemble the real ones. In the second case the element of rhythmic manipulation is important.

1a. Parallel fifths caused by a dissonant passing tone. The vertical relationship that the dissonant passing tone bears to other voices is accidental and insignificant, as evidenced by the fact that it belongs to no chord. Hence, parallel fifths are permissible when one of the tones is a dissonant passing tone, as in Example 245.

Ex. 245

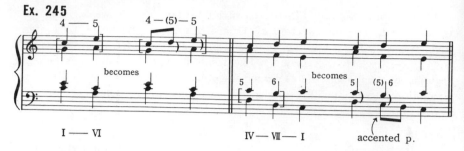

I — VI   IV — VII — I   accented p.

1b. Parallel fifths caused by a consonant passing tone. The consonant passing tone, because it agrees with all of the voices that accompany it, is vertically responsible for its interval relationships. The parallel fifths that it creates with other voices are, in miniature, like parallel fifths created solely by chord tones. Because consonances are always heard as vertically significant intervals, such parallel fifths are doubtful. For our own purposes they occupy an intermediate position between original chordal fifths which are to be avoided and fifths created by a dissonant passing tone which are permissible. Whether they are to be allowed or not depends finally on the situation in which they occur. The questions that should be answered before creating such a situation are:

a. Is the chordal succession so clear that the real relationships can assert themselves, thus subordinating the superficial fifths?

b. Are there less dubious means that serve the same purpose?

In Example 246, the excerpt from Josquin contains parallel fifths caused by the motion of a consonant passing tone, and that from Bach avoids the fifths in a similar situation by interchanging the voice parts. Example 246*c* illustrates other ways of circumventing such fifths.

Ex. 246[3]

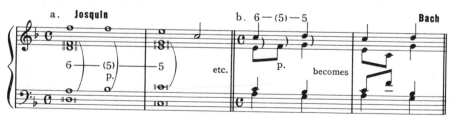

[3] Ex. *a,* Josquin Després, *Wereldlijke Werken,* Volume II, page 56, bars 17–18.

Ex. *b,* Bach, "Herr, wie du willst, so schick's mit mir," bar 2.

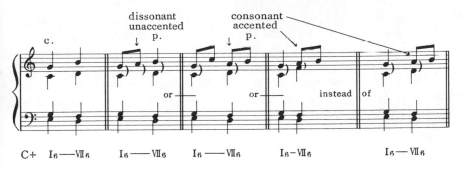

Example 247 illustrates two ways of decorating a chord sequence. Example *b* has no fifths but Example *c*, with its accented passing tone, has three pairs of fifths, the first caused by a consonant passing tone. The fifths in the Mendelssohn example are caused by the interpolation of a chromatic passing tone, C–sharp. The two bars illustrated are part of a more inclusive 5–6–5 technique, as indicated in the sketches of Example *d*.

Ex. 247

4 Ex. *e*, Mendelssohn, op. 54, Variations sérieuses.

Occasionally, to maintain an even rhythm, a passing tone may be increased in its time value. In Example 248 parallel fifths result from the use of this technique. The example from Bach illustrates how a passing tone equal in conception to a sixteenth note becomes an eighth note in execution. That from Rosenmüller illustrates a similar change from an eighth note to a quarter note. The Bach example contains a dissonant passing tone, the Rosenmüller a consonant one.

Ex. 248

2. *Parallel fifths corrected by passing tones.* We shall now direct our attention to the ways in which passing tones interpolated between chordal fifths can restore the independence of voices. As already pointed out, rhythm more than consonance or dissonance plays a decisive role.

The accented passing tone is a more effective agent in breaking up parallel fifths than the unaccented passing tone. The reason for this is that the accented passing tone prevents the simultaneous sounding of the tones that comprise the second of a pair of fifths, which the unaccented passing tone cannot do.

In Examples 249*d* and *e,* the unaccented passing tones are too incidental in nature effectively to break up the successive fifths which each pair of chord tones strikes simultaneously. The accented passing tone, however, shifts one of the tones that comprise the second fifth, and this is enough to insure independence of part writing.

Ex. 249

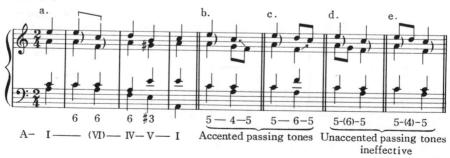

[5] Ex. *a,* "Jesu, der du selbsten wohl," bar 15.

  Ex. *b,* "Welt, ade!" bars 13–14. No. 350 in *Johann Sebastian Bach's Werke,* Volume VII, Breitkopf und Härtel, Leipzig.

Parallel octaves, unisons, and the passing tone

Parallel octaves and unisons caused by passing tones are to be avoided. Parallel octaves, because they stand for nothing more than tones and their identical duplications, always create the impression that two performing voices are doing the work of one, and this fact alone is sufficient to destroy independence of voices. The same is true in the case of parallel unisons. In fact, it is only in a situation where chordal parallel octaves already are present that passing tones which are an octave apart can be introduced, as indicated in Example 250.

Ex. 250

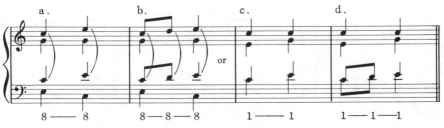

Therefore, as long as our aim is to write for four independent voices, parallel octaves and unisons are to be avoided. Although the perfect fifth comprises closely related tones, it is at least made up of essentially different tones so that incidental parallel fifths are permissible where parallel octaves and unisons are not.

The insertion of a passing tone, accented or unaccented, will not correct already existent parallel octaves or unisons. The tones that comprise parallel octaves and parallel unisons are in too strong and binding a relationship to be broken up by so incidental an interpolation as a passing tone.

Ex. 251

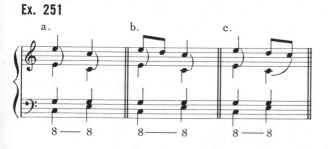

Passing tones in the minor mode

The only problem that the minor mode presents for the use of passing tones is centered about the manipulation of the sixth and seventh steps, the variable tones, in order to avoid the melodic progression of an augmented second.

1. When the sixth and seventh steps are used successively as passing tones in the interval of a fourth, raise both steps in ascending and retain the lowered form of both steps in descending.

Ex. 252

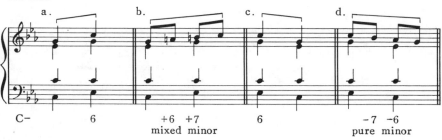

2. When either the sixth or the seventh step is a chord tone, the form, raised or lowered, of the passing tone should be the same as that of the chord tone, regardless of whether the motion is ascending or descending.

Ex. 253

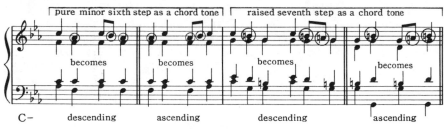

THE NEIGHBORING TONE

Description

The neighboring tone (n.) as a detail of figuration may be used in all of its forms, complete and incomplete, accented and unaccented.

Ex. 254

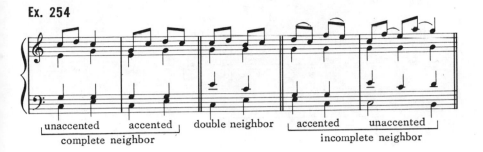

unaccented   **accented** | **double neighbor** | **accented**   **unaccented**
complete neighbor   **incomplete neighbor**

The chromatic lower neighbor

At times the chromatically altered lower neighbor, because of its more active melodic relationship to the principal tone, may be used successfully instead of the diatonic lower neighbor.

Ex. 255

a. Diatonic Neighbors

b. Chromatic Neighbors

Parallel fifths caused by neighboring tones

As discussed earlier in connection with passing tones, parallel fifths caused by a dissonant neighbor are permissible, while those caused by a consonant neighbor are doubtful.

Ex. 256

Dissonant Neighbor (permissible)

Ex. 256 (cont'd)

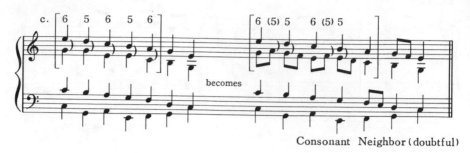

Consonant Neighbor (doubtful)

Parallel fifths corrected by neighboring tones

Like the accented passing tone, the accented neighbor breaks up real fifths by shifting one of the tones involved in the faulty relationship.

Ex. 257

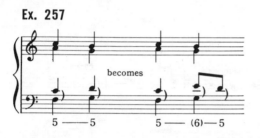

The unaccented neighboring tone is better equipped to break up fifths than the unaccented passing tone because it can break up the single motion into two shorter motions.

Ex. 258

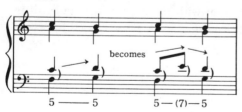

Parallel octaves, unisons, and neighboring tones

The neighboring tone in any of its forms is not capable of breaking up real octaves or unisons; and octaves or unisons produced by the motion of neighboring tones will destroy the independence of part writing.

Ex. 259

Summary of the Relation of Figuration Tones to Parallel Motions

For purposes of summarizing the discussion of parallel motion, Example 260 and 261 illustrate the various elements of figuration which, by their insertion between chordal parallel fifths, octaves, or unisons, preserve independence of voices.

A. Elements effective in breaking up chordal parallel fifths:

Ex. 260

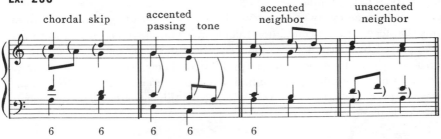

B. Elements effective in breaking up chordal parallel octaves and unisons:

Ex. 261

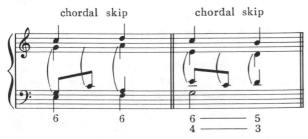

The permissible parallel fifths are those in which one of the tones is a passing tone or a neighbor, both preferably dissonant.

Ex. 262

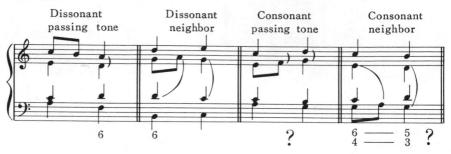

The most important interval relationships are those formed by the bass against the soprano. These outer voices set the framework of musical activity by their composite motion. They should be kept as free as possible of faulty motion. The inner voices, as they form relationships either between themselves or with one of the outer voices, fill in this framework; it is in the intervals that they form that occasional fifths or octaves may be covered by the use of tones of figuration.

It has been necessary to discuss problems of voice leading at such length in this chapter that a misconception might understandably be formed as to the role played by tones of figuration. They are not used merely to create or break up parallel motions hitherto prohibited. Their primary missions are to add rhythmic, melodic, and motific interest to exercises and to afford linear ways of providing triads with color. It is with this in mind that experiments should be made with them.

EXERCISES WITH TONES OF FIGURATION

Proceed with exercises as before; that is, fill in the chord tones before attempting to insert decorative tones. When this has been accomplished, seek out the natural opportunities for inserting tones provided by the voices as they move from one chord tone to another. A passing tone may be inserted in the interval of a third (Example 263*b*). A stationary or repeated tone may be decorated with a neighbor (Example 263*a*, also *i,* soprano). A chordal skip, or a neighbor, may be applied to stepwise motion (Examples *e,* bass; *g,* alto; *h,* soprano; and *d,* soprano) or to the larger intervals (Example *d,* bass). When tones are inserted in more than one voice at a time, care should be exercised to establish some relationship between them. Most certain of success are those simultaneously moving tones in parallel thirds and sixths,[6] for in such cases the voices reinforce each other's motion (Examples *c, d, g,* and *i*). At complete V-I cadences it is best to preserve the definitive leap from the root of V to the root of I (Examples *e* and *g*). Sometimes this leap may be filled in with passing tones (Examples *i* and *f,* bass). Finally, experience will teach that grammatical correctness alone in the application of tones of figuration does not assure their musical success. A summary of the figuration tones introduced in the present study appears at the end of Chapter 14.

Ex. 263

6 Review Ex. 112.

Ex. 263 (cont'd)

14

Tones of Figuration, Rhythmic

Suspensions and anticipations are figuration tones of rhythmic origin. They differ from chordal skips, passing tones, and neighbors, which have melodic origins. The former cease to be suspensions and anticipations when certain rhythmic conditions, to be described, are not fulfilled. The latter, on the other hand, depend on the fulfilling of the melodic conditions already described. But we shall see that rhythmic figuration tones have a melodic value, just as melodic figuration tones have a rhythmic value.

THE SUSPENSION

Description

The suspension (s.) arises out of a delaying or shifting of the normal rhythmic motion of a voice. Example 264*a* illustrates a progression with all voices moving in a normal rhythm. The remaining examples illustrate forms that the suspension takes: in Examples *b* and *c* the suspension grows out of a delaying of the completion of the soprano motion C-B; in Examples *d* and *e* the soprano motion is shifted or syncopated; the suspended tone may be tied as in Examples *b* and *d*, or repeated as in *c* and *e*, the difference being one of execution and not one of principle.

Ex. 264

The suspension grows out of a succession of two tones. Because the first tone is either lengthened or shifted, the complete process takes place in three acts involving the initial tone, its suspension, and the succeeding tone. Each of these tones plays a definite role in the process that creates a suspension. The initial tone prepares the way, its suspension precipitates a feeling of tenseness, and the final tone releases the tension and returns the situation to normality. The successful operation of these functions depends on metric position, voice leading, and doubling, each of which will be discussed in the following paragraphs.

The metric position

The suspension falls on a beat or fraction of a beat that is stronger than that of the succeeding tone. In only this relationship of beats can the climax be rhythmically precipitated and then released. The position of the initial tone is variable.

Ex. 265

Initial tone Susp. Succeeding tone

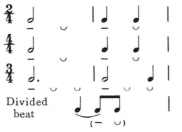

Voice leading

There are two kinds of suspensions: those that form consonant relationships with the other voices and those that form dissonant relationships, as illustrated in Example 266.

Ex. 266

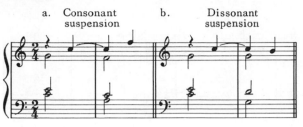

a. Consonant   b.   Dissonant
   suspension   suspension

In both cases the initial tone and the suspension are identical. The consonant suspension is free from further restrictions. The dissonant suspension is characterized by stepwise motion to the succeeding tone.[1] There are two possibilities of stepwise motion, descending and ascending. Of these two, descending is the more natural. This follows from the climactic nature of the suspended tone as compared with the following tone which provides the denouement or release. The suspended tone is the high point of action; the succeeding tone stands for falling action.

Resolution by stepwise motion upward takes place in those situations where attending circumstances, such as harmonic expectancy and the normal motion of a tone, demand it. In the progression V or VII$_6$-I, when the leading tone is suspended, its resolution must be by stepwise motion upward because stepwise motion downward would bring about a chord different from I.

Ex. 267

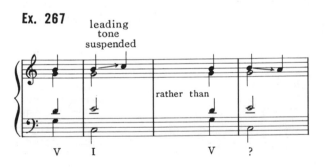

leading
tone
suspended

rather than

V   I   V   ?

The upward resolving suspension is more certain of success when it is reinforced by a suspension in another voice resolving by either upward or downward motion, as in Example 268.

---

[1] Review in Chap. 4, *Consonance and Dissonance.*

Ex. 268 [2]

Doubling

The dissonant suspension, as can be seen by examining Examples 264 and 268, operates in such a way that an essential chord tone, the tone of resolution, is delayed in its arrival. It is this delay that creates a feeling of tension. Poor doubling can very easily interfere with the success of the effect. The suspension operates most clearly when the tone of resolution is not doubled (Example 269b). It operates least clearly when it is doubled in the unison (269g). The reason for this, which also suggests a remedy, is that by doubling the tone of resolution, it appears in one voice in a normal rhythm before it appears in delayed fashion in the suspended voice (as in 269d and g). The resolution is thus obstructed because the goal of its motion has already been reached in another voice. The remedy (Examples 269e and h) is to forestall the premature arrival of the doubled tone of resolution by suspending in both voices, if possible. If this does not work effectively, change the doubling.

Ex. 269

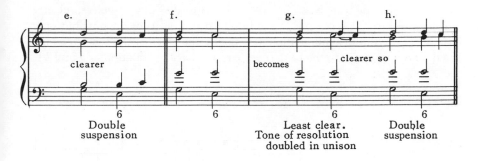

Suggested uses of the suspension

A few examples will illustrate how the three considerations of rhythm, voice leading, and doubling operate when the suspension is introduced into a chord succession. In the connection IV-I in Example 270, suspensions may be introduced into either the tenor or the alto, both of which move stepwise downward; or they may be introduced simultaneously into both voices. The soprano, because it is stationary, and the bass, because it skips, cannot be treated with suspensions. In Examples *b* and *d*, the suspensions create the illusion of chords. These are pure accidents, by-products of the operation of suspensions. As such they have no harmonic meaning. Study the voice leading, the doubling, and the metric position of the suspension and the resolution.

Ex. 270

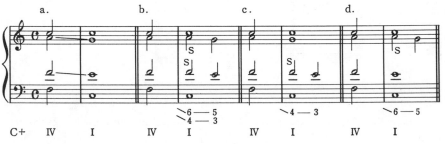

In Example 271 the problem is one of selecting the best of three possible choices for the introduction of a suspension. All of the voices are equally well placed as far as metric position is concerned. Beyond this, the bass, because its motion is downward, is better than the soprano, and because the tone of resolution is not doubled, it is better than the tenor. Note how the bass repeats from a weak to a strong beat as a result of suspending the C. This does not interfere with a clear statement of the metric position of the succession because the bass, in its clash with the upper voices, clearly demonstrates that it is occupying the first beat not on its own rights but only because, by rhythmic manipulation, it is taking the place of the tone B, which has the original claim to the beat (compare the basses of Examples *a* and *b*).

Ex. 271

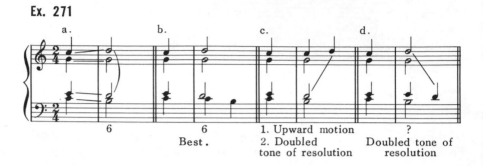

6	6	1. Upward motion	?
	Best.	2. Doubled tone of resolution	Doubled tone of resolution

The demands of harmonic succession at times make it necessary to double the tone of resolution in the octave. For example, in the cadential progression V-I (Example 272), the necessity of placing I in root position is strong enough to take precedence over any possible criticism of a doubled tone of resolution (see also Example 268*b*).

Ex. 272

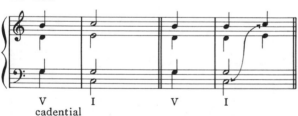

V   I   V   I
cadential

Octave doubling is best when: (1) it is the root of the chord; (2) some further end is served. Thus the bass, often obliged to express specific tones for harmonic reasons, is the voice that doubles in the octave in most cases. Middle voices can usually be modified to avoid such a doubling.

Following are the clearest dissonant suspensions. Study the voice leading and doubling.

Ex. 273

Parallel fifths corrected by suspensions

The dissonant suspension is one of the most valuable techniques that break up real parallel fifths. The principle of operation is similar to that of the accented passing tone in that the second of the pair of fifths is changed by it from a vertical to an oblique relationship, as illustrated in Example 274.

Ex. 274 [3]

[3] Ex. *b*, Bach, "Der du bist drei in Einigkeit," bar 1. See also "Herr Jesu Christ, wahr'r Mensch und Gott," bars 4–5.

Ex. *f*, Haydn, London Symphony, first movement.

The indirect suspension

The indirect suspension (in. s.) differs from the normal suspension only in the relationship of the initial tone to the suspended tone. In the normal suspension the initial tone and its suspension appear in one and the same voice. In the indirect suspension the initial tone appears in one voice and its suspension appears in another. As can be seen in Example 275, the indirect suspension is like the accented incomplete neighbor in effect. In Example *b* the initial tone appears in the tenor, but it is suspended in the soprano.

Ex. 275

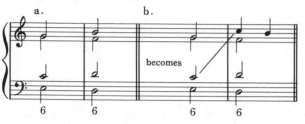

The indirect suspension is an important device in situations where there is no opportunity to use the normal downward resolving suspension. In Example 276*b* the alto suspends and resolves the tones that appear in the soprano, leaving that voice free to ascend.

Ex. 276

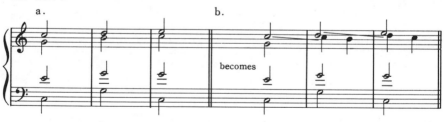

The decorated resolution

The relationship between the dissonant suspension and its resolution is so strong that a decorative chordal skip or neighbor may be interpolated without creating a disruptive effect, as in Example 277.

Ex. 277

Chordal skips   Neighbors to tone of resolution

Suspended passing tones and neighbors

The rhythmic pattern of the suspension may be applied to the passing tone and the neighbor. This device works to advantage in that it changes a three-tone succession into a four-tone one. Thus in decorating a melody, four half beats may be represented by a tone apiece whereas before only three had a note apiece. This is shown in each pair of illustrations in Example 278.

Ex. 278

THE ANTICIPATION

Description

The anticipation (a.) is the rhythmic opposite of the suspension. As its name suggests, it is a tone that is struck in advance of the beat on which it would normally be played. Its effect is the opposite of that of the suspension in that it heralds or prepares the way for an approaching chord. To do this properly it should fall on a beat weaker than that of the tone for whose entrance it prepares the way. The anticipation may be tied to the following tone.

Ex. 279

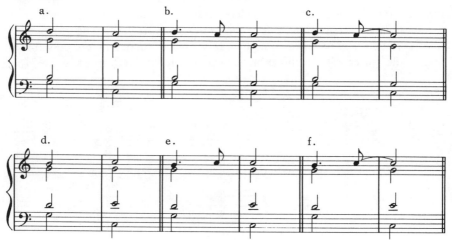

The dissonances created by the anticipation are automatically explained by the later arrival of the beat and tones with which it belongs. Hence there is no precaution of voice leading that must be heeded as in the case of the suspension. Furthermore, the rules of doubling need no special manipulation here. They operate as they generally do.

Direct and indirect anticipations

In the direct anticipation illustrated in Example 279, the anticipation and the anticipated tone appear in one and the same voice. In the indirect anticipation (in. a.) the relationship is shared by two voices. In effect the indirect anticipation is like the unaccented incomplete neighbor.

Ex. 280

Parallel fifths caused by the anticipation

Parallel fifths caused by the use of an anticipation are superficial, just like those caused by the dissonant passing tone and neighbor. In Example 281*b*, the parallel fifths are negligible in that the second pair is comprised of an anticipation and a passing tone.

Ex. 281[4]

Parallel fifths corrected by the anticipation

The anticipation may be used to break up real parallel fifths by anticipating one tone of the second pair of fifths as in the two quotations from Bach in Example 282.

---

[4] "Freuet euch, ihr Christen alle," bar 2. Also bars 4, 6, and 16. See also "Jesu meines Herzens Freud'," bar 12.

Ex. 282[5]

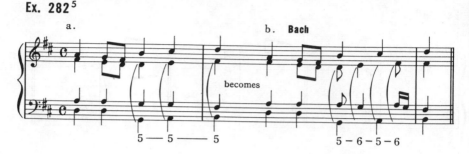

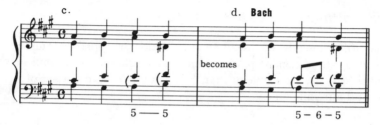

WEAK-STRONG REPETITIONS IN THE BASS

The suspension and anticipation are, as we have seen, rhythmic manipulations of the metric scheme: the suspended tone is held or shifted beyond its normal length, the anticipated tone arrives, or is shifted, ahead of its normal beat. The one looks backward and the other forward for its normal metric position. Weak-strong repetitions in the bass are correct when we can feel that either of these processes is taking place. Example 283 illustrates the weak-strong operation of suspensions and anticipations in the bass of the succession stated in the first part.

Ex. 283

[5] Ex. *b*, "Jesus, meine Zuversicht," bar 1.
    Ex. *d*, "Freu dich sehr, O meine Seele," bar 1.

with anticipations in the bass

The rhythmic principles of the suspension and anticipation, when applied to the entire chord, very often produce weak-strong repetitions in the bass. Example 284*a* shows a connection of four chords in a normal metric order. By lengthening the first chord the subsequent ones are shifted beyond their normal positions (Example *b*). In Example *c*, each chord except the first anticipates its true metric position.

Ex. 284

SUMMARY—CHAPTERS 13 AND 14

In developing a terminology for tones of figuration, our guides have been explicit meaning and the specific relation to surrounding harmonies. For these reasons, the general term "tones of figuration" seems more appropriate than the widely used "nonharmonic" tones. Rhythmic tones of figuration are simply shifted "harmonic" tones, and consonant melodic figuration tones actually create a momentary chord, or as in the case of chordal skips, lead their lives entirely within a prevailing chord. None of these is "nonharmonic," but they do add elements of figuration to a ground plan.

Our specific terms have been built up from two generally applicable terms of the sixteenth century: *transitus* for passing tone, and *ligatura* for suspension. Such frequent terms as appoggiatura and échappée reflect specific stylistic practices, rather than a logical derivation. Observe, in Example 285, that the term appoggiatura appears six times. It means "leaning note" and simply denotes a condition of accentuation. But the student of musical texture should be interested in describing exactly the factors that bring about the "leaning," hence the need to distinguish among the six cases. The same criticism can be made of échappée (escaped note), which appears twice. In Example 285, a list has been made of the terms that have been introduced into Chapters 13 and 14, along with abbreviations and roughly equivalent terms of wide use.

Ex. 285

TONES OF FIGURATION

Term	Abbreviation	Other Terms
A. Of melodic origin		
Chordal skip	c. s.	Arpeggio, Broken chord
Neighbor	n.	Auxilliary
Neighbor, accented	ac. n.	Appoggiatura
Neighbor, double	d. n.	Changing notes
Neighbor, incomplete	i. n.	Cambiata, échappée
Neighbor, incomplete, accented	i. ac. n.	Appoggiatura
Passing tone	p.	Transitional note
Passing tone, accented	ac. p.	Appoggiatura
B. Of rhythmic origin		
Anticipation	a.	None
Anticipation, indirect	in. a.	Échappée
Suspension	s.	Appoggiatura, prepared Appoggiatura
Suspension, indirect	in. s.	Appoggiatura

Example 286 illustrates each kind as it is introduced into a simple context.

Ex. 286

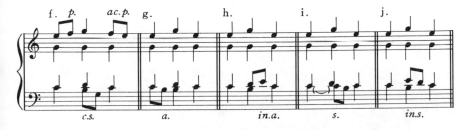

15

Sevenths

Descending and ascending passing tones may be manipulated to the point where they become identified with the chord that accompanies them. In this manner, chords of four or more tones may be formed. The process, partly rhythmic, partly melodic, is in brief:

Ex. 287

Because the manipulation in Example *a* fits so well into the descending natural succession, we shall call the four-tone chord which is formed by it the chord of the seventh, and turn our attention to it alone for the time being. Later, we shall study the type illustrated in Example *b,* called the pseudo seventh. The difference between the two chords lies not in their construction but, as always, in their behavior.

THE CHORD OF THE SEVENTH

Positions

Example 288 illustrates the relationship between the triad and the chord of the seventh with respect to positions, figured bass indications, and

the location of the new tone. Although we call the dissonance a seventh, its distance above the bass varies with the positions of the chord. It lies a seventh above the bass only when the chord is expressed in $\frac{5}{3}$ position, now called $\frac{7}{5}$. When the chord is in the $\frac{6}{3}$ position the dissonant tone lies a fifth above the bass (new signature $\frac{6}{5}$); and in the $\frac{6}{4}$ position, a third above ($\frac{4}{3}$). Finally it may itself appear in the bass to form a new position, $\frac{6}{4}$.

Ex. 288

Triad positions

Positions of the chord of the seventh

Chords of the seventh in root position

The deficient diminished fifth that makes the expression of diminished triads a precarious venture is so effectively covered by the seventh that when this tone is added such chords may be used in root position. They are VII⁷ in the major mode, II⁷ in the pure minor mode, and VI⁷ and VII⁷ with raised roots in mixed minor (consult Example 300*e* and *f*).

Voicing leading

a. The guiding rule of voice leading for the correct treatment of the chord seventh is that the new tone resolves by *stepwise motion downward.*

Ex. 289

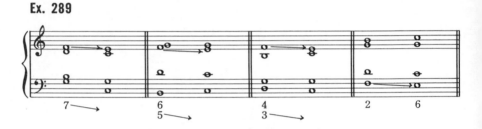

The reason for this important restriction of the motion from a chord seventh will become evident later when the origin and uses of the new tone are discussed.

b. The interval progressions 2–1, 9–8, and 7–8 sound awkward more often than not in four-part writing and should be avoided.

Ex. 290

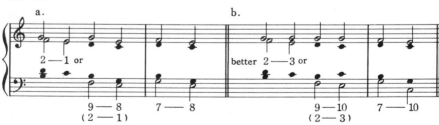

The awkwardness of the examples in 290*a* is apparent when they are compared with those in 290*a*. In Example *a* the empty octave and unison sound weak after the dissonant second, ninth, and seventh. In Example *b*, on the other hand, the full, harmonious tenth and third are much more capable of absorbing the preceding intervals. In terms of four voices the following examples in *a* are hazardous and should be avoided; those in *b* are free of criticism:

Ex. 291

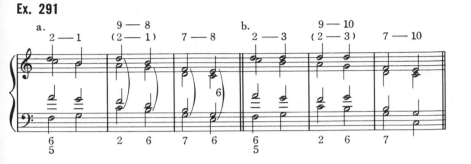

In more complex styles where the emptiness of the unison and octave can be covered by the freer play of rhythm and motive, such resolutions occasionally take place, but even here rarely between the outer voices (Example 292).

Ex. 292[1]

Schubert

c. The use of the chord seventh presents on occasion a threat to independence of voice leading in that it increases the danger of writing parallel fifths.

Ex. 293

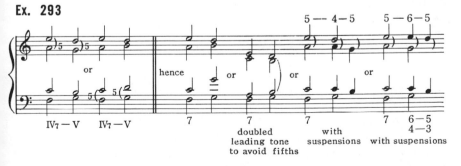

----

[1] Schubert, Tänze, Op. 53, No. 33.

Doubling

Ordinarily the four tones of the chord of the seventh may be so distributed that each voice expresses one of them with no tone doubled.

Ex. 294

Certain conditions of voice leading may make it impossible at times to express a complete chord. In such cases the root should be doubled and the fifth omitted. In Example 295 such a doubling averts parallel fifths.

Ex. 295

Furthermore, the obligatory downward resolution of the seventh and attendant problems of voice leading lead frequently to a following incomplete chord, with the fifth omitted.

Ex. 296

Use of sevenths in chord progressions

In applying sevenths to triads it is well to keep in mind that there are only two progressions to which the new tone may be added with a fair assurance of success:

a. In progressions that involve roots a descending fifth apart (or an ascending fourth) ; that is, whenever the descending natural succession is employed, a seventh may be added to the first chord.

Ex. 297

The chords may stand in various positions.

Ex. 298

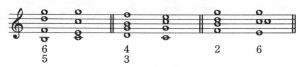

b. In progressions that involve roots an ascending second apart, a seventh may be added to the first chord.

Ex. 299

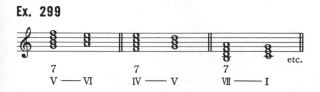

Extensions of these two progressions will be treated later in the section on prolonged sevenths.

Qualities of seventh chords

As long as there is an opportunity to resolve them properly, sevenths may be added to any chord. Example 300 is a table of qualities of seventh chords in major and minor.

Ex. 300

In order to compare these qualities more conveniently, Example 301 presents the various qualities of chords of the seventh built from a common root.

Ex. 301

Origin and Uses of the Chord Seventh

At a time when the employment of dissonances is the rule of the day, it might seem wasteful to give more than passing attention to the chordal seventh. Yet there is a rationale behind the musical use of all dissonances, and in many cases it is similar to the rationale that underlies the use of the chordal seventh. As we discuss its origin and uses, we shall be developing two skills; an understanding and command of seventh chords and an understanding and eventual command of more complex dissonant sonorities.

Basic to our approach is the technique of replacement, whereby a foreign tone, having been associated with a chord, eventually usurps the place of a tone native to the chord. In the case of the chord seventh, the new tone is a replacement of the duplication of the root, as in Example 302.

Ex. 302

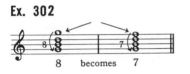

It is this specific kind of replacement that distinguishes the characteristic chord seventh from other sevenths that will be discussed later.

The most frequently used sevenths are those added to the primary chords I, IV or II, and V. But the origin of the seventh is the same whether applied to the chords that are close to the key center or to the more remote chords.

As an enlarged passing tone

The seventh comes about often through a rhythmic enlargement of a downward moving passing tone and its consequent replacing of the duplication of the root.

Ex. 303

As Example 303*c* indicates, the passing tone F, which replaces the duplication of the root G, retains its character as a passing tone, for it still moves from G in I to E in I.

This derivation of the seventh as a rhythmically enlarged passing tone may be applied to dependent chords. Compare Example 304 with Examples 131 and 132. The sevenths appear in the inner voices:

Ex. 304

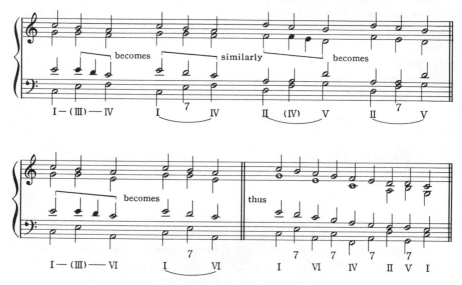

A study of the preceding examples of seventh chords and an understanding of their dependent origin will reveal why, in hearing them, we judge them correctly to be vertical incidents rather than independent, harmonic chords. In the examples that have to do with the relationship between I and (III) the total impression is not of two separate chords but of a single chord, I, which is presented first in its original form and then in action. The motion in the bass from C to E is less like a leap from root to root than a leap from a root to the third of the same chord (Example 305).

Ex. 305

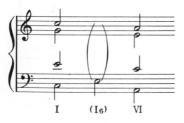

But with this leap in the bass there appears a complex of passing tones.

Ex. 306

The incidental vertical nature of this complex of tones is more apparent when the bass and upper voices assume other forms.

Ex. 307

Much more definitive in these examples than the vertical identity of each group of tones is the tendency of horizontally conceived tones such as passing tones to move in thirds and sixths from one point to another.

In order to explain the origin of increasingly dissonant phenomena, we proceed from simple consonant situations to the manipulations that create dissonances. We have already seen that not all sonorities have equal harmonic rights. The most important reason why vertical names are given to dependent chords, such as (III), is for convenience in locating and discussing them. As soon as their positions and uses have been mastered it is better to become unburdened of their applied vertical names and think more in terms of interval relationships and ways of moving from point to point. The bane of the study of harmony is a mind cluttered up with vertical names that are only by-products of motion rather than its cause. The significant vertical combinations are those that mark the beginnings and ends of motions.

As a neighbor

The seventh frequently replaces the duplication of the root to create the effect of a neighbor, either complete or incomplete.

Ex. 308

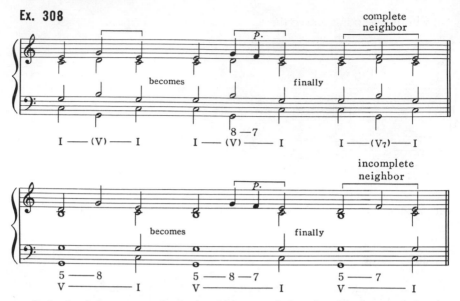

In both of these examples it should be noted that the chord seventh has its origin as a descending passing tone. The melodic elision of the source of its activity and its consequent rhythmic enlargement make it into a neighbor when heard in its final context. The seventh may appear in any voice. Compare Example 309 with Examples 180 and 182.

Ex. 309

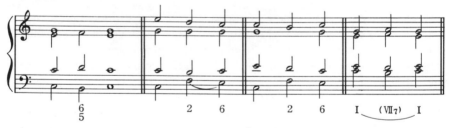

The seventh as an incomplete neighbor may replace the chordal skip as a means of breaking up direct parallel fifths. Compare Example 310 with Examples 242c and 258.

Ex. 310

As a direct suspension

A useful way of winning a chord seventh is through the operation of the principles of voice leading characteristic of the suspension. As indicated in Example 311*a*, the descending passing tone is rhythmically enlarged to displace G, the original beginning of its motion. The metric position of the suspended tone is variable. Examples *b*, *c*, and *d* illustrate a combination of the seventh as a passing tone and as a suspension. The interpolated chords serve as a consonant preparation for the dissonant suspended sevenths. Compare Example 311 with Examples 269 and 273. Note in the earlier examples that suspension and resolution occur over the same bass note, but in Example 311 the bass changes. This is a significant difference between the simple suspension and the suspension of a chord seventh.

Ex. 311

A few examples will suffice to illustrate applications of this technique of winning a seventh.

Ex. 312

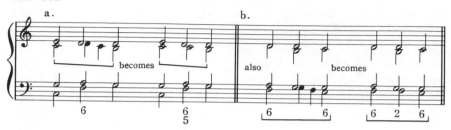

A combination of these two examples leads to a way of obtaining sevenths in consecutive chords, a technique that may be designated as interlocking or overlapping sevenths.

Ex. 313

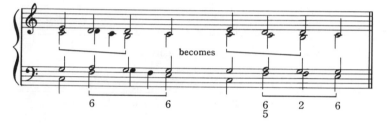

This technique is used by Bach in the opening bars of the first prelude in the *Well tempered Clavier*, Book I.

Ex. 314

The following examples illustrate more extended applications of this technique to the descending natural succession. The arrows indicate the stepwise downward resolution of each seventh. Compare Example 315 with 121.

Ex. 315

An examination of the outer voices of the preceding examples will reveal the guiding relationships that set the plan of motion.

Ex. 316

Thus, even the natural succession of bass tones is closely related to a technique of voice leading.

Various positions are used in Example 317. The suspension may appear in any pair of voices.

Ex. 317

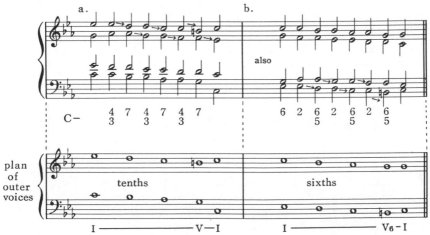

This technique represents a more complex four-voiced form of the 5–4–5 suspension technique as illustrated in Example 274*e* and *f* which, with its accompanying text, should be reviewed.

Ex. 318

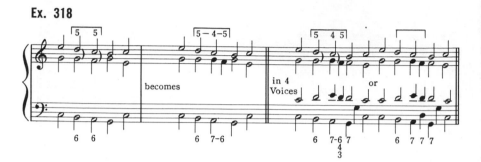

An examination of the interval relationships formed by the two upper voices and the two lower voices in Example 317*a* and *b* will reveal more extended application of 5–4–5 successions.

As an indirect suspension

The indirect suspension of a seventh is in effect like the seventh used as an incomplete neighbor.

Ex. 319

Other examples of the same technique follow. The arrows connect each initial tone with its suspension as a chord seventh.

Ex. 320

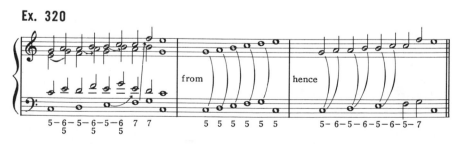

The introduction of a seventh as a suspension in the first few chords above adds a new detail to a succession whose real motivating principle is the outer voice interval relationship 5–6–5. This was discussed and illustrated in Example 176*b* and *c*, which should be compared with Example 320.

Summary

The preceding discussion of the characteristic uses of the seventh chord has uniformly illustrated the derivation of the new tone from a descending passing tone. Through the operation of the principles of melodic replacement and rhythmic enlargement, the seventh forms new horizontal associations which make it into an enlarged passing tone, a complete or incomplete neighbor, and a direct or indirect suspension. Its origin more than its applied uses accounts for its stepwise descending resolution.

EXPANDED TREATMENT OF THE SEVENTH

The relationship between the seventh and its resolution is so binding that certain manipulations are possible. These are classified as the decorated resolution, the transferred seventh, the transferred resolution, and the prolonged seventh.

The decorated resolution

The first of these occurs when melodic ornaments are interpolated between the seventh and its resolutions.

Ex. 321

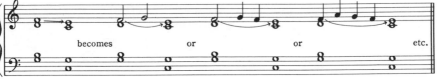

Example 322 illustrates applications of this melodic device.

Ex. 322²

In the minor mode the upper neighbor to the lowered sixth step is always the lowered seventh step, even when the raised seventh step is used as a chord tone in another voice. The difference in the function of each of the tones, one as a neighbor and the other as a chord tone, excludes the relationship from the realm of the cross relation.[3]

Ex. 323

The transferred seventh

Like all tones that are identified with a chord, the seventh may be transferred from one voice to another before its normal resolution takes place. The seventh resolves only on the arrival of the succeeding chord (Example 324).

[2] Ex. 322a, Mozart, K 494, bars 95–98.
   Ex. 322b, Bach, *Well tempered Clavier*, Bk. I, Fuga XXIV, bar 32.
[3] Review in Chap. 11, *The cross relation*.

Ex. 324[4]

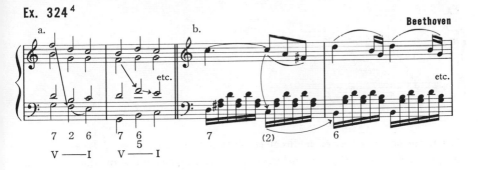

The transferred resolution

The transferred resolution arises when the seventh appears in one voice and the resolution in another. The most frequent employment of such a device aims to win a complete chord where the normal entrance and resolution of the seventh in one and the same voice would not accomplish this.

Ex. 325[5]

Example 325*a* illustrates first the normal resolution of the seventh and the resultant incomplete chord, and then, in *b*, the sharing of the seventh and the resolution by two voices, which leaves the alto free to move to the fifth of the following chord. The Beethoven excerpt above shows a more extended treatment of the same device. Note the proximity of the voices involved in the transfer of the resolution, which consequently takes place in one register. The success of a transfer is less certain in four-part writing when the voices are further apart.

---

[4] Beethoven, Sonata, Op. 2, No. 3, last movement.
[5] Beethoven, Sonata, Op. 14, No. 2, 2nd movement.

Ex. 326

On those occasions when a direct resolution leads to 2–1 or 7–8, as in Examples 290 and 291, a transferred resolution, regardless of the register, should be tried as a possible alternative to abandoning the use of the seventh (Example 327).

Ex. 327[6]

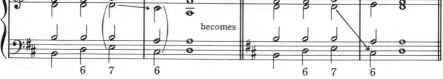

In Example 328a the factors motivating the use of a transferred resolution are the interval succession 7–8 and the incomplete chords that result from normal treatment of the seventh (Example 328).

---

[6] Ex. 327d, Bach, "Liebster Immanuel."

Ex. 328[7]

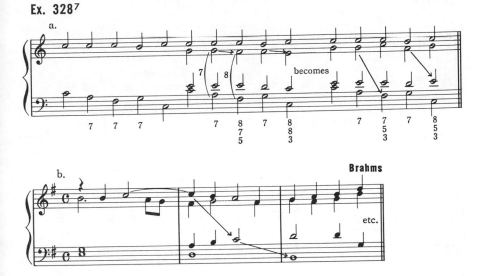

The transferred resolution is not so uniformly certain of success as the direct resolution, for the dissonant tone must always overcome its first tendency to resolve by descending in the voice in which it appears. It is best employed when the voice to which the transfer is made accompanies the voice with the seventh in parallel thirds or sixths. A review of Examples 325*b* and *c* will illustrate this.

The prolonged seventh

We have seen how incidental decorative notes interpolated between a chord and its successor often form consonances that take on the appearance of chords. These horizontal contributions to music are of prime importance and give to it much of its wealth of detail. The highest vertical rank they ever reach is that of dependent chords. They should always be heard as details rather than as goals of motion. When such tones of figuration are interpolated between a chord of the seventh and its succeeding chord, the seventh does not resolve immediately but awaits the appearance of its real successor. The interpolated intervals, regardless of their nature, do not discharge the tendency of the dissonance to resolve by stepwise motion downward.

[7] Ex. 328*b*, Brahms, Op. 29, No. 2.

Ex. 329

These characteristic interpolations between V^7 and I are simple incidents of figuration having no effect on the resolution of the seventh. A frequent interpolation and consequent prolonging of the seventh occurs in the succession $II^{\overset{6}{5}}$ or $IV^7\text{-}V^{\overset{6-5}{4-3}}$.

Ex. 330

The Beethoven excerpt (Example 331) is a good illustration of such a prolonged seventh. Chromatic passing tones, G–flat and A–natural, are inserted between $II^{\overset{6}{5}}$ and $V^{\overset{6-5}{4-3}}$ (Example 331).

Ex. 331[8]

plan

Eb+   II$\frac{6}{5}$

Beethoven

$\frac{6}{4}$ —————— $\frac{5}{3}$

V ————————————— I

Example 332 contains additional illustrations.

Ex. 332

also

$\frac{6}{5}$ (6) 7   7 $\natural\frac{6}{5}$ $\binom{6}{4}$ 7 $\natural\frac{4}{3}$ $\binom{8}{\natural5}$ $\natural\frac{6}{5}$ $\binom{6}{4}$ 7

C+ II ————— V I   C— VII ——— I   I — VII ————————— I

[8] Beethoven, Sonata, Op. 31, No. 3, 1st movement, beginning.

DISSONANT MELODIC LEAPS

The use of seventh chords, with their dissonant interval content, affords an opportunity to experiment with dissonant melodic leaps, principally those that form sevenths, diminished fifths, augmented and (in the minor mode) diminished fourths, and (also in the minor mode) the augmented second. Certain typical causes of such leaps may serve as guides to their application.

1. Circuitous or decorated melodic motions that are substituted for original, simpler successions frequently result in dissonant skips.

Ex. 333

2. Related to such motions are those cases in which one performing voice outlines the functions of two voices.

Ex. 334

3. Dissonant leaps are frequently caused by the transposition of a melodic succession from one register to another.

Ex. 335

4. The augmented second may be tried as an alternate to the use of the pure minor or the raised sixth and seventh steps, to whose employment considerable attention has already been given. The Examples that follow illustrate the use of the augmented second as a detail of motion from the fifth to the eighth steps.

Ex. 336

It is customary to avoid the augmented second melodically for stylistic reasons in harmonizing chorale melodies. The writer could find only one such interval in the 371 Bach Chorales published by G. Schirmer (Example 337).

Ex. 337 [9]

On the other hand, in the choruses of the Cantatas and, of course, in his instrumental works, Bach uses the augmented second freely.

Dissonant melodic leaps are not to be judged as good or bad by themselves alone, but in terms of their function, in terms of what they accomplish as details of a more inclusive melodic pattern.

PSEUDO POSITIONS

Introduction

As already indicated in Example 287, not all active tones have the same origin as the chordal seventh. Therefore, not all are obliged to follow the principle of stepwise downward resolution. In the following section an examination will be made of those vertical results of voice leading which look like positions of the chord of the seventh but whose context reveals a difference in origin and use. In order to distinguish such apparent vertical combinations from the real positions of chords of the seventh, we shall call them pseudo positions. In most cases the simple rather than the manipulated operation of tones of figuration causes the apparent position.

Pseudo sevenths

The operation of simple tones of figuration frequently creates pseudo sevenths (Example 338).

---

[9] Bach, "Nun lob' mein' Seel'," bar 20–22.

Ex. 338 [10]

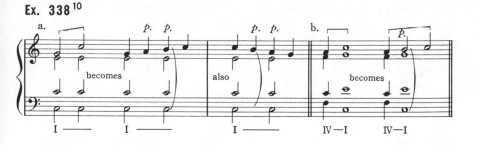

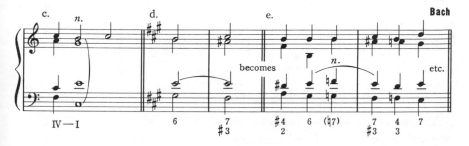

A pseudo seventh is at times created by a neighboring tone motion in the middle voices and the support given it by the bass.

Ex. 339

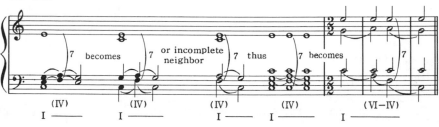

In all of the illustrations of example 339 the seventh created by the bass and soprano has nothing in common with the chordal seventh. In the chordal seventh it is the manipulation of the upper tone of the interval that forms

[10] Ex. 338*e*, Bach, "Es ist genug."

the seventh and its consequent activity that creates the situation; here it is the figuration and activity of the lower voices that create the interval. The E which is retained throughout is the representative of the tonic chord, and its retention indicates the more clearly the incidental and dependent nature of the inner voices and the bass.

Ex. 340 [11]

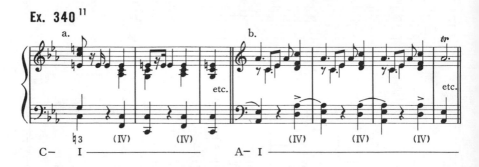

In both of the excerpts of Example 340 the neighboring tone motion of the middle voices and the support given to it by the bass create the pseudo seventh.

The pseudo six-five

Passing and neighboring tones that lie a sixth above the bass of a $\frac{5}{3}$ create the pseudo $\frac{6}{5}$ position (Example 341).

Ex. 341 [12]

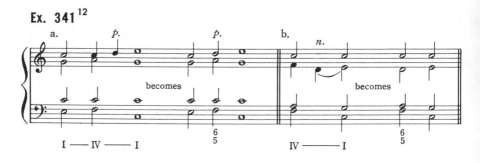

[11] Ex. 340a, Chopin, Mazurka, Op. 56, No. 3, closing bars.
      Ex. 340b, Chopin, Mazurka, No. 51 (no opus No.), closing bars.
[12] Ex. 341c, Brahms, Quartet, Op. 51, No. 2, 3rd movement, bars 10–12.

In the pseudo $\frac{6}{5}$ position, it is the activity of the *sixth* above the bass as a passing tone or a neighboring tone that creates the dissonance. In the real $\frac{6}{5}$ it is the activity of the *fifth* that accounts for the position.

The pseudo four-three

The pseudo $\frac{4}{3}$ is created in its most characteristic form by ascending passing tones that lie a third above the bass.

Ex. 342

The pseudo six-four-two

The pseudo $\frac{4}{2}$ is most characteristically created by the motion of neighboring tones or passing tones above the bass.

Ex. 343

Summary

In all pseudo positions the basis of activity is different from that which brings about the more characteristic real positions. In order to clarify this distinction, pseudo and real positions are juxtaposed in Example 344. Study in each case the voice whose activity causes the dissonance directly or indirectly. This activity is indicated by means of arrows in the figured bass symbols.

Ex. 344

In general, where the *upper* tone of a seventh *descends* in chords of the seventh, the *lower tone ascends* in pseudo positions. (See Example 287). Another distinguishing feature of the real chord of the seventh is root movement by a descending fifth (as in V^7-I) or by an ascending second (as in V^7-VI).

Ex. 345

Chords of the 7th   Pseudo 7ths

The organ point

Characteristic of the origin of pseudo positions is the use of retained tones, chord tones that are held or repeated while tones of figuration carry out one or another task. The organ point is a retained tone applied to the bass. Built most frequently on either the tonic or the dominant steps of the scale, it acts as a support for the harmonic or figurational activity in which the upper voices engage. Like all retained tones, the intervals it forms with the active voices above it are incidental and not furctional in the sense of chordal sevenths. In Example 346, illustrating the tonic organ point, the upper voices should be disengaged from the bass except at the beginning and end of each example, where all voices define a chord. Note how the presence of the organ point casts over the entire succession a feeling of the supervisory presence of I, whose root it is.

Ex. 346[13]

[13] Ex. 346*c*, Schubert, Tänze, Op. 18 No. 2.
Ex. 346*d,* Beethoven, Bagatellen, Op. 33, No. 1.

Ex. 346 (cont'd)

Conclusion

Chordal sevenths, as we have seen, are a result of the application of certain specific linear and rhythmic techniques to triads. Such sevenths, requiring stepwise downward resolution, are to be distinguished from those that result from processes described in the preceding section. Pseudo positions occur in so many situations that only a suggestion of the principles giving rise to them can be described. One final example will summarize the distinction between functional chordal sevenths and these others. The excerpt from a Mazurka by Chopin was chosen to demonstrate a relation between plan and an execution which includes chromatic elements.

In the first part a broad outline is presented which, in the succeeding sketches, assimilates the various technical factors that give the passage its individuality. As indicated in Example 347*a*, the harmonic scheme is I-IV-V-I with the seventh of V being introduced as a suspension. This is the only real seventh in the entire excerpt. In 347*b*, IV is introduced by a chromatic passing chord. In 347*c*, *a* neighboring 4–3 is followed by three 7–6 suspensions. The previously noted chordal seventh, D, is resolved by D-C in bars 9–10, actually the repetition of bars 1–2.

Example 347*d* reveals highly individual touches. Note that I (in bar 2) expresses F rather than E in the middle voice. This unusual nuance characterizes the Mazurka throughout the first part, as well as at the beginning and end of the entire piece. In all cases the sonority stands for a tonic chord, which is made apparent by the bass. Note that the excerpt includes four sevenths and two six-four-twos. Only one of these, V7, as already noted, is a real seventh chord; the others are products of simple neighboring and suspension techniques.

Ex. 347

In comparing the sketches of Examples 347 with 348, observe that the 7–6 techniques are carried out directly by the middle voice. The top part is released for elaborations in the form of neighbors that assume fanciful extensions in subsequent phrases, which should be examined.

Ex. 348 [14]

---

[14] Ex. 348, Chopin, Mazurka, Op. 17, No. 4, bars 5–14.

Ex. 348 (cont'd)

SUMMARY

Context must be consulted as a means of determining which treatment of a seventh is in use in each case. The tones that create a seventh may be part of:

1. A chord of the seventh with
   a. Normal resolution
   b. Extended treatment in the form of a:
      1. Decorated resolution
      2. Transferred seventh
      3. Transferred resolution
      4. Prolonged seventh
2. A pseudo seventh formed by
   a. Tones of figuration
   b. An organ point

16

Ninths

Ninths, like sevenths, arise in two ways: as simple and as manipulated tones of figuration. The latter, which we shall call the chordal ninth, will be discussed first.

As a manipulated tone of figuration, the chordal ninth is won as a prolonged suspension which completely replaces the duplication of a chordal root.

Ex. 349

THE CHARACTERISTICS OF NINE-SEVEN

An examination of Example 349 will reveal the following details of treatment of ninth chords:

1. The ninth, like the seventh, resolves by stepwise motion downward.

2. It is usually accompanied by the chord seventh, with which it moves in parallel thirds or tenths.

3. The roots of the ninth chord and the following chord are a descending fifth apart (V-I). Hence, they represent the descending natural succession.

4. The chord fifth is omitted in four-part writing, leaving four tones, one for each voice.

5. The interval of the ninth is formed by the outer voices, but its upper tone may also appear in inner parts. When the ninth appears in middle voices, it plays an accompanying role whose chief value comes from the way in which it moves in thirds or sixths with the seventh.

Ex. 350

When the ninth is reduced by an octave to become a second, a less clear relationship results, directly related to the 2–1 suspension.[1]

Ex. 351

For the sake of clarity in part writing, we shall avoid such a progression. Of course, the second formed by the inversion of a seventh does not share this opaqueness, for it is related to the 2–3 suspension. There is no obstructive anticipatory presence of the tone of resolution in the register in which the resolution takes place.

[1] Review in Ch. 15, *Voice leading*, part *b*.

Ex. 352

THE APPLICATION OF NINE-SEVEN

The descending succession

The ninth may be added as a prolonged suspension to all chords, whether principal or dependent.

Ex. 353

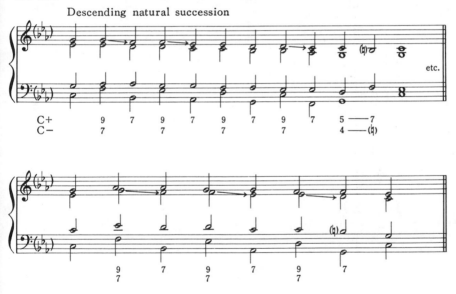

The smooth execution of interlocking ninths demands five voices. So long as we restrict ourselves to four-part writing, such a technique remains outside our province.

Ex. 354

V Nine-Seven

V_7^9 is a combination of tones that has constructive features shared by no other $_7^9$. Actually it is a fusion of two closely related chords, V^7 and VII^7, both of which contain the same diminished fifth and succeed readily to the same chord, the tonic.

Ex. 355

The peculiar nature of V_7^9 accounts for the frequency of its use, particularly with the ninth added as a neighbor.

Ex. 356

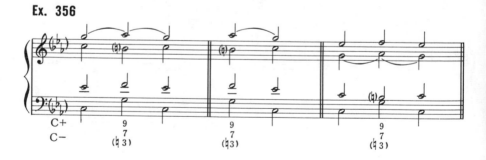

The circumstances that surround the construction of this chord act as a guarantee of safe conduct for the ninth. It is frequently used melodically over the dominant chord to parallel a melodic leap of a fifth in the tonic chord, as in Example 357.

Ex. 357²

The details of construction and succession that identify the V_7^9 are not to be found in any other $_7^9$. The result is that neighboring tone motions that create the intervals $_7^9$ on any degree other than the dominant lack harmonic identity. They remain details of horizontal motion, vertical accidents in more definitive surroundings. The following examples should be heard as taking place in single chords with simple elements of figuration accounting for the activity of the upper voices. Example 358c combines a chordal leap in the bass with passing tones in the upper voices.

2 Ex. 357*b*, Schubert, Op. 50, No. 18.
  Ex. 357c, Schubert, Op. 9, No. 34.

Ex. 358[3]

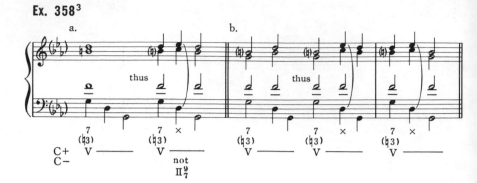

Brahms

FURTHER CONSIDERATIONS OF THE NINTH

Pseudo ninth chords

The functional chordal ninth is characterized by complete replacement of the duplication of a chord root through the operation of a prolonged suspension. It should be distinguished from those ninths that only temporarily replace a chord tone and resolve to it before the underlying chord

---

[3] Ex. 358*e*, Brahms, "Des Abends."

has been quitted. Such ninths are nothing more than simple tones of figuration and represent the unmanipulated operation of passing tones, neighboring tones, suspensions, and anticipations, as in Example 359.

Ex. 359[4]

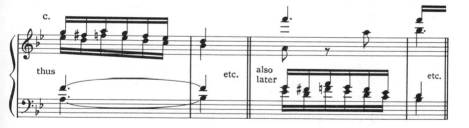

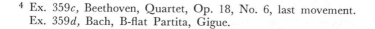

---

[4] Ex. 359c, Beethoven, Quartet, Op. 18, No. 6, last movement.
Ex. 359d, Bach, B-flat Partita, Gigue.

Sustained chord tones frequently form ninths against tones of figuration in accompanying voices. In such cases the principle of resolution which applies to chordal ninths does not operate. The ninth in the following examples comes about through the use of a passing tone in the bass, accompanied in thirds by the tenor against a held soprano chord tone. Compare Examples 360 and 138*d*.

Ex. 360

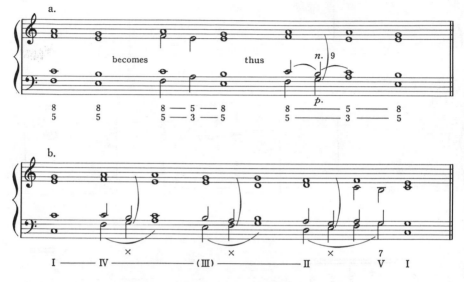

Related to the preceding example is the following, in which the sustained chord tones in the soprano leap to the succeeding tones. Again, the incidental passing tone ninths formed by the active bass against the soprano have nothing in common with functional chord ninths.

Ex. 361

Chordal leaps occasionally form incidental ninths against held tones, as illustrated in Example 362. A V-I connection with simple suspensions over I is illustrated in Example 362*a*. In Example *b* the bass breaks through E on the way to C. The E stands for the third of the tonic chord and not for a III$^9_7$. Compare Examples 362*e* and 138*d*.

Ex. 362[5]

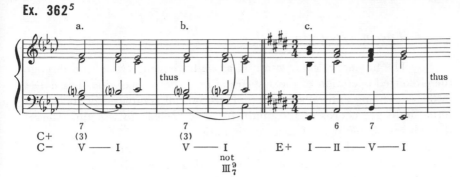

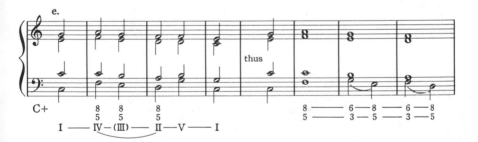

[5] Ex. 362*d*, Brahms, Op. 118, No. 6, bars 1–2.

The inverted ninth

The functional chord ninth is, as we have seen, a tone won through the prolonged operation of the suspension in a chord succession that moves in the descending natural succession. Thus, not all complexes of tones that form ninths are chords of the ninth, for it is possible to win the interval through the simple play of tones of figuration.

The ninth as a chord tone invariably appears above the root of the chord, which in its turn lies in the bass. If, in working an exercise, a combination of tones should be hit upon that seems to be an inverted chord of the ninth, the chances are that it is a result of simple figuration as in Example 363, which represents a passing tone motion, with additional decorations, through a tonic triad. Observe the parallel motion in tenths between the outer voices.

Ex. 363[6]

A frequent case such as the following brings to the fore VII^7 more than V_7^9. At most it represents a dependent chord with a sustained tone in the tenor. Actually it is nothing more than a cluster of neighboring tones.

[6] Ex. 363*e*, Schumann, Op. 99, No. 11, Trio.

Ex. 364[7]

Successions such as the following are nothing more than neighboring tone motions, the constructive features of which come from the parallel leading of voices in thirds and sixths. Uninverting them in order to make dominant ninths of them is a waste of time.

Ex. 365

CONCLUSION

Most of the ninths that are heard in music are caused by the play of tones of figuration. They have little to do with harmonic meaning. The *inverted* "ninth chord" is a fiction, for with sonorities such as those in Example 365, stronger factors dominate. These factors are, as usual, contextual and horizontal. In Example 365, the principal C chord forms the prime context. The horizontal factor is parallel motion in thirds and sixths. These account for the alleged ninths more directly and, quite important, more simply than the cumbersome mechanism of "inverting" and "uninverting."

---

[7] Ex. 364*b*, Schubert, Op. 9, No. 30.

Many dissonant sonorities are accounted for by the technique of replacement. As indicated in Example 366a, the "eleventh" arises as a replacement of the third and should be regarded simply as a fourth, rather than as an eleventh. Similarly, the "thirteenth" (366b) is, in fact, a sixth that replaces, or occasionally graces the fifth.

Above all, the conduct of the bass is of paramount importance in judging tonal skyscrapers. Observe in Example 366c that the bass in one case denotes V-I, but with the same seven tones rearranged it denotes IV-I. Inversion here is out of the question.

The manipulations that create such dissonances can often be traced to unique rhythmic, motific, or voice leading factors. Examples 366d to f present model illustrations of such activating techniques. They bring about, in bar 3 of the excerpt, two arresting sonorities. Example 366d presents a simple sketch which shows each tone in its proper place in a harmonic environment framed by II moving to V. Example 366e illustrates a persistent C in the top voice, based on the chorale melody that Bach was setting. The C replaces the normal B which arrives late.

The elaborate figuration of Example 366f is characteristic of the entire Chorale Prelude. Note the extension of the bass relationship, A to B, by way of a downward motion that starts in the second part of bar 1, picks up a $\frac{6}{3}$ over E in bar 2, and reaches its goal, B, at the beginning of bar 3. There can be no meaningful talk of III[9] or I[11] in the first inversion for the sonorities of bar 3, for they have a direct origin in the texture of the piece itself rather than in such harmonic assumptions.

Ex. 366 [8]

[8] Ex. 366f, Bach, Orgelbüchlein, "In Dir ist Freude."

17

Applied Dominant Relationships

In this chapter we shall consider conditions under which the diatonic tones of a key become chromatically altered. Our discussion will be limited to those chromatic changes that are made on diatonic chords in order to endow them with the color of characteristic dominant-tonic progressions; namely, V or VII-I, successive dominant chords, and I-V.

Two important factors are chord quality and root progression. Because these two considerations must cooperate in all uses of such techniques, we shall call the process, "Applied Dominant Relationships." The term "Secondary Dominants," often used in the same sense, is not satisfactory, for it places the stress on only one factor, chord quality, while overlooking the equally important one of chord behaviour.

It will be helpful to summarize the various qualities of V, VII, and I chords. Example 367 describes the diatonic forms and qualities of V and VII chords in root position.

Ex. 367

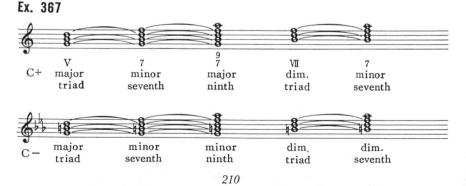

	V	7	9 7	VII	7
C+	major triad	minor seventh	major ninth	dim. triad	minor seventh

	major triad	minor seventh	minor ninth	dim. triad	dim. seventh
C−					

As indicated in Example 368, tonic triads are either major or minor, but never diminished in their original form.

Ex. 368

C+   I
  major triad

C−   I
  minor triad

THE APPLICATION OF V-I AND VII-V

Description

Any major or minor triad, regardless of its step name—that is, regardless of whether it is actually II, III, IV, and so on—may be approached as if it were a tonic triad. In order to create this effect it is necessary to precede it by its own V or VII; that is, it must be approached by a major chord whose root lies a perfect fifth above it (its own V) or by a diminished chord whose root lies a minor second below it (its own VII).

Ex. 369

7
V ——— I

7
VII ——— I

Observe the succession VI-II in Example 370.

Ex. 370

I ——— VI ——— II ——— V ——— I
                         7

The root of VI lies a fifth above (or, inverted, a fourth below) that of II. Hence, we are in a position to give to the succession a V-I color. The only chromatic change necessary is that from C to C-sharp in VI. It will become a major triad, and II will be approached as if it were the tonic triad of D minor as in Example 371. The application of such a color as this does not rob the succession of its original harmonic meaning, which is determined by its environment. VI-II in a C major context will continue to operate as VI-II regardless of the applied color as long as the surrounding bass tones and chords assert that key, as they clearly do in this case.

Ex. 371

The two chords involved need not stand in root position. The addition of the seventh to the applied dominant adds conviction to the succession. Note the larger C major context in the motion of the outer voices.

Ex. 372

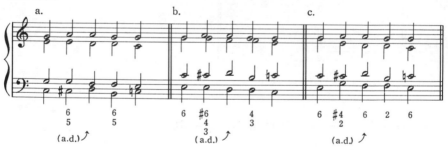

The color VII⁷-I may be applied to a succession such as that in Example 373, in which the roots (I⁷-II) stand a major second apart. Two chromatic changes are necessary. Since II is a minor triad, its own VII⁷ will be a diminished seventh whose root lies a minor second below that of II. The succession of roots as they now stand, C-D, must be changed to C-sharp—D, a minor second; further, the vertical interval C-sharp—B (bass-alto), a minor seventh, must be made into C-sharp—B-flat, a diminished seventh.

Ex. 373

Example 374 below illustrates this VII⁷-I color applied to the same succession in other positions.

Ex. 374

Note in all of the examples that the chromatic changes are applied to the chord that assumes a dominant color and that the chord to be addressed as a tonic remains unchanged.

Construction and voice leading

1. *Doubling.* Because applied dominant chords contain the same kind of leading tone one finds in all dominant harmonies, they are subject to the same precautions of doubling. Therefore, do not double the third of an applied V or the root of an applied VII. These sensitive tones are not always recognizable through the presence of a preceding accidental, for at times two diatonic tones of a chord must be chromatically altered, and at other times the momentary leading tone remains in its original diatonic form. As a guide to the many new leading tones, Example 375 presents each chord of C major, first in its diatonic form, and then in the forms of an applied V and an applied VII. Each of these latter is followed by the chord to which it is addressed as a form of V or VII. The momentary leading tone is notated as a whole note in each case and slurred to its momentary tonic. In studying the example

observe the following points: a) In 375a, E (whole note) is not chromatically altered, but C-sharp is. Neither should be doubled. The same point should be observed throughout the example; b) The applied dominants appear with sevenths throughout. The applied VII chords appear sometimes as diminished triads, at other times as diminished seventh chords, the latter when use of the diminished seventh requires no additional accidental. c) For the time being, IV (375d) produces no applied V, and VI (375f) no applied VII. The reason is that the momentary tonic to which these might be addressed is a diminished triad and not approachable through a form of applied dominant.

Ex. 375

Example 376 presents the same kind of summary for the minor mode.

Ex. 376

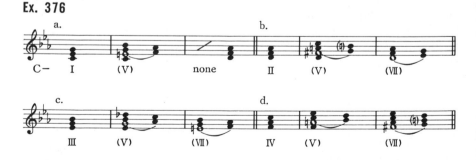

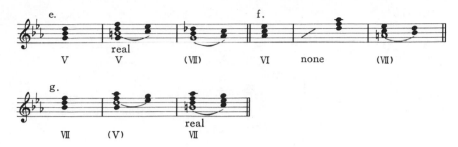

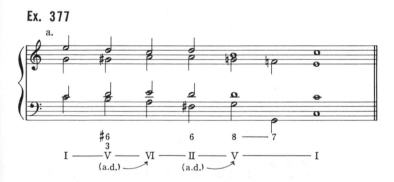

2. *Chromatic progressions.* Use of applied dominants presents many opportunities to write chromatic successions, such as the C to C-sharp of Examples 371 to 374. As discussed in Chapter 11 in the section *Chromatic
Progressions,* the second tone of such a succession cancels the first tone most
effectively when both tones are assigned to the same voice and register.

Not all altered tones are reached through chromatic half steps. In Example
377, two altered notes are introduced; G-sharp and F-sharp. Only the first
of these is preceded by the diatonic form of the same note, hence, the complete progression has been placed in the alto. F-sharp, however, is reached by
a leap in the bass because F is not present immediately before the entrance of
the altered tone; thus the problem of a chromatic succession does not arise.

Ex. 377

Example 378 is presented in three stages: first, as a direct three-part progression; then with an extending element consisting of parallel sixth chords
between I_6 and II_6; and finally with applied dominant relationships. Note
that chromatic successions are placed in a single part and register.

Ex. 378 [1]

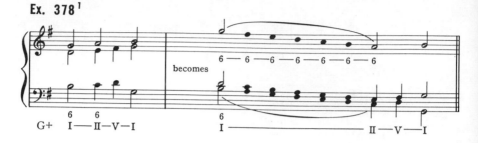

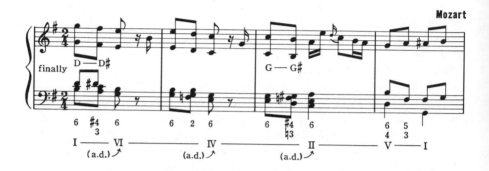

When the diatonic tone is doubled before its chromatic alteration as in Example 379, place the altered tone in one of the two voices and, if possible, lead the other voice away by stepwise motion. Example 379a prevents more successfully than Example b a lingering impression of the alto G after the entrance of G-sharp in the bass. Consult Examples 371 and 373 for further illustrations of the treatment of doubled tones.

Ex. 379 [2]

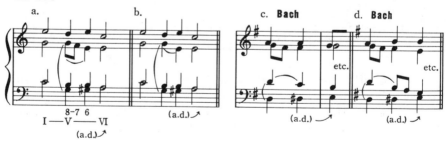

[1] Mozart, Sonata, K 311, 2nd movement.
[2] Ex. 379c, Bach, Chorale, "Lobt Gott," bars 7–8.
    Ex. 379d, Bach, Chorale, "Meines Lebens letzte Zeit," bar 14.

When one of the doubled tones lies in the soprano, it is generally better to place the chromatically altered tone in that voice. The melodic nature of the chromatic passing tone makes it more adaptable to the uppermost voice (Example 380).

Ex. 380

In Example 381 from Schumann, motific considerations lead to the allotting of the chromatic motion to the middle voice and the leap to the soprano. The skip of a fourth is characteristic of the upper voice throughout the composition.

Ex. 381[3]

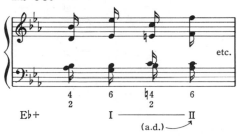

3. The cross relation. Chromatically altered tones are most simply introduced as passing tones, but it is not always possible to apply them in this way. Just as simple diatonic plans of voice leading are frequently changed to more complex forms, so do chromatic successions appear in forms other than that of a chromatic passing tone. In the three-voice Example 382, a simple 5-6-5 succession is presented in its original form and then with an interchange of parts. Compare the bass and tenor of Example *a* with Example *b*.

---

[3] *Bunte Blätter*, Op. 99, No. 5.

Ex. 382

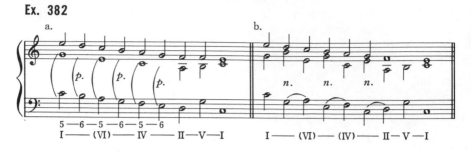

Note that the passing tones in the bass of Example 382*a* give way to neighboring tones in Example *b* as a result of the interchange of parts. Dominant color may be applied to both of these examples. In the case of Example 383*a,* the chromatic alterations appear as passing tones in the alto with an implicit completion of their motion (thus G–G-sharp–[A] in the first three chords and C–C-sharp–[D] in the fifth, sixth, and seventh). In the case of Example *b,* the diatonic tone and its alteration, which acts as a neighbor, appear in different voices and registers, thus forming cross relations.

Ex. 383

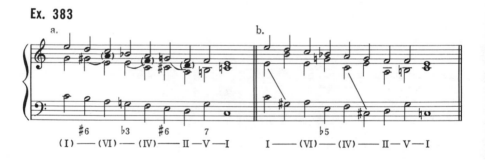

Example 384 expresses similar cross relations.

Ex. 384[4]

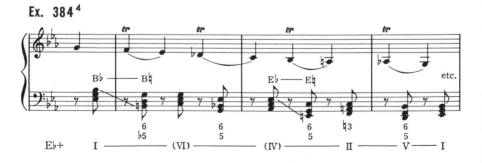

[4] Beethoven, Sonata, Op. 31, No. 3, 1st movement.

Here too, the separation of the diatonic tone from the chromatic alteration in both voice and register comes as a result of an interchange of parts. Compare Example 385 with the beginning of 384.

Ex. 385

Our aim here is not to prohibit employment of the cross relation but to establish an order of procedure to be followed whenever a chromatic succession of tones is used. The first choice should be to introduce the succession in the simplest and most natural manner. In brief, place the diatonic-chromatic succession in one voice and register. When it is not possible to do this, according to the plan of voice leading, consider the possibility of the cross relation. That is, place the diatonic tone in one voice and the succeeding chromatic tone in another.

The sudden clash that arises occasionally when the cross relation is employed can be mollified by inserting passing chords, or simply passing tones, in one or both of the voices involved (Example 386).

Ex. 386[5]

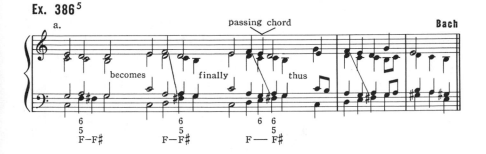

---

[5] Ex. 386*a*, "Herzlich thut mich verlangen," bars 11–12.
 Ex. 386*b*, "Die Sonn' hat," bar 4.
 Ex. 386*c*, "Christus, der uns selig macht," bars 2–3, transposed.

Ex. 386 (cont'd)

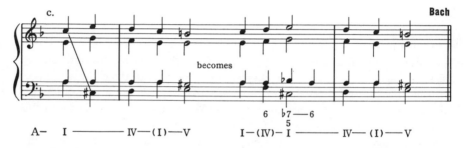

The following examples are also from Bach. Note the use of passing tones.

Ex. 387[6]

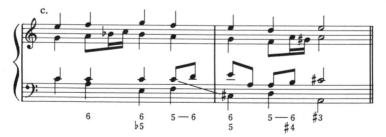

[6] Ex. 387*a*, "Gott hat," bars 3–4.
Ex. 387*b*, "Christus, der uns selig macht," bars 13–14.
Ex. 387*c*, "Freu' dich sehr," bars 5–6.

Example 388, illustrates skips to and, in *b*, from the tones involved in a chromatic succession.

Ex. 388[7]

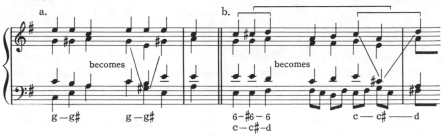

Diminished seventh chords (VII^{♭7})

In addressing major triads through their own VII[7] it is sometimes to the advantage of the connection to construct VII[7] as if it were going to move to a minor triad.

Ex. 389

In the major mode, root and seventh of the VII[7] form a minor seventh; in the minor mode, a diminished seventh. Hence, the seventh is a half step lower in the minor mode than in the major.

Ex. 390

The lowering of the seventh increases its activity toward the tone of resolution.

[7] Ex. 388*a*, "Ach Gott, wie manches Herzeleid," bar 9–10.
Ex. 388*b*, "Jesu meine Freude," bars 9–10.

Ex. 391

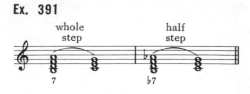

The following examples illustrate characteristic uses of this relationship. Note the horizontal employment of the seventh as a chromatic passing tone in Example 392*a* and, in Example *b*, the sequential advantage of A-flat–G over A–G, after B-flat–A.

Example 392*c* illustrates the minor mode or diminished seventh form of VII[7] applied to IV, a major triad, and subsequently the minor mode form of VII[7] in C major.

Ex. 392

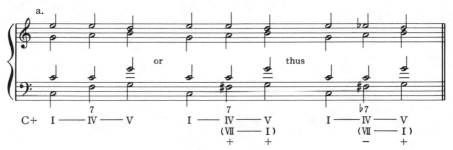

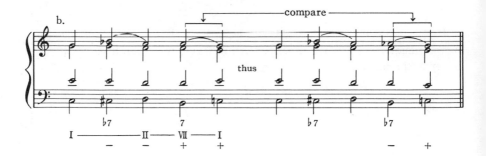

The general principle behind such successions is that of mixtures; that is, the original major mode progression is supplanted by one making use of elements of the minor mode.

SUCCESSIVE DOMINANT CHORDS

The technique underlying the use of consecutive dominant color is that of interlocking or overlapping sevenths (review Example 315). The process of elision grows out of the natural succession.

Ex. 393

Starting with VII in Example 393, each chord is presented successively in two forms; first as a triad and then as a dominant seventh. The elision of the triad form of the chord leads to the construction of Example 394.

Ex. 394

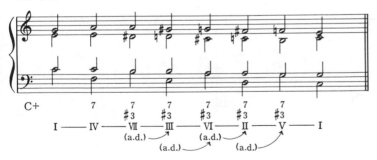

A common application of this technique is to be found in the connection II-V-I or IV-V-I.

Ex. 395

In Example 395a the chromatic succession is placed in one voice. In Example b the succession is shared by two voices, the bass and the alto. The chromatic succession is placed in one voice in Example 396.

Ex. 396[8]

The same applies in the case of Example 397.

Ex. 397[9]

[8] Ex. 396, Beethoven, Sonata, Op. 2, No. 2, 1st movement.
[9] Chopin, Valse, Op. 64, No. 2.

In Example 398 the chromatic succession is divided between two voices and registers. Study the relationship between the harmonic plan with its soprano arpeggio, G-C-E, and the excerpt. The $^6_5$ in the second bar is a neighboring chord. In bars six and seven the chordal succession IV⁷-II$^6_5$ is veiled by the motific alternation E-D in the soprano. Instead of E alone in bar six and D alone in bar seven, both tones appear in each of the bars.

Ex. 398 [10]

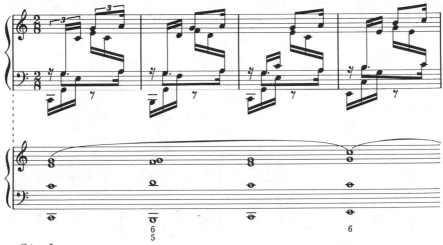

---

[10] Chopin, Prelude, Op. 28, No. 1.

An interpolated $^6_4$ resolving to $^5_3$ between a chord that has assumed dominant color and the succeeding chord is a quite frequent practice, particularly at cadences in the succession II (or IV)-V-I (Example 399).

Ex. 399[11]

THE APPLICATION OF I-V

The application of the color I-V may be used when the succession of roots stands in the relationship of an ascending perfect fifth (or, inverted,

11 Ex. 399*b*, Schubert, Op. 9, No. 32.
   Ex. 399*c*, Schubert, Op. 9, No. 29.

a descending perfect fourth). Again, the chord that is altered is that which assumes the color of a dominant (Example 400).

Ex. 400[12]

C+   I   (V   II)   VI
#3
(a.d.)

Schubert

etc.

IV   V   6 ———— 7   I
                  4 ———— 5
                        3

SUMMARY

A. The principles.
   1. Any major or minor chord may be preceded by its own V or VII
      (Examples 371–374, etc.).
   2. Any major or minor chord may be succeeded by its own dominant
      (Example 400).
   3. A dominant may be succeeded by the dominant whose root lies a
      perfect fifth below (Examples 394–399).
B. Construction of V and VII chords.
   1. V.
      a. Its root lies a perfect fifth above (perfect fourth below) that of the
      chord to which it is addressed (Example 369).
      b. Its quality is major with a minor seventh. The ninth, major or
      minor, may be included (Example 367).
   2. VII.
      a. Its root lies a minor second below that of the chord to which it is
      addressed (Examples 369, 389).
      b. Its quality is diminished. The minor or diminished seventh may be
      included (Example 367, 389–392).
C. Doubling.
   1. Do not double the third of an applied V (Examples 375, 376).
   2. Do not double the root of an applied VII (Examples 375, 376).

D. Voice leading.

   1*a*. The simplest way to express a half step succession is to place both tones in the same voice and register (Examples 377, 378, 383*a*, 385*a*).

     b. If the diatonic tone is doubled, introduce the chromaticized successor into one of the voices and, if possible, lead the other away by step (Examples 371, 373, 379–381).

   2. The cross relation occurs when the chromatic succession is divided between two voices (Examples 383*b*, 384, 385*b*, 386–388). It is a concomitant of increased complexity of voice leading.

18

Modulation

The study of modulation embraces, first, the ways in which keys are related, second, the process of moving from one key to another, and third, modulation in its relation to form.

RELATIONSHIP OF KEYS

The principles that govern key relationships are an enlargement of those that govern the relationships of chords. The *harmonic* nature of chords is determined by the distance, in fifths, of their roots from the tonic chord.[1] The *horizontal* nature of chords is determined by the precise way in which they arise as details of motion from one point to another. Chords in both of these senses serve to create and express a key. Modulation expands chordal relationships to the degree where a chord contributes not merely itself to musical expression, but all the characteristics of the key in which it is a tonic. For example, C major may be expressed by the *chord* progression, tonic (I)–dominant (V)–tonic (I), or by the *key* progression, tonic key (C+)–dominant key (G+)–tonic key (C+). Both progressions express identical functions; the former in smaller and the latter in larger values.

A distinction must be drawn between the various keys to which modulation may be made and the tonic key, the key of a composition. In the same sense that the tonic key has supervised and been served by its tones and chords, it now supervises and is served by keys. Its meaning, therefore, is more inclusive than the meaning of the other keys. This greater inclusiveness is signified by the term, *tonality.* Thus a composition with its entire complex of tones, chords, and keys is said to be in the tonality of the tonic key.

[1] Review in Ch. 8, *Root Progression by Fifths.*

Of all the keys that are related to a tonality, our concern here is with those that show close kinship. These are the keys whose tonic triads reside as diatonic chords in the tonality. In the case of C major the most closely related keys are G major, D minor, A minor, E minor, and F major, all of whose tonic triads lie in the key of C.

Ex. 401

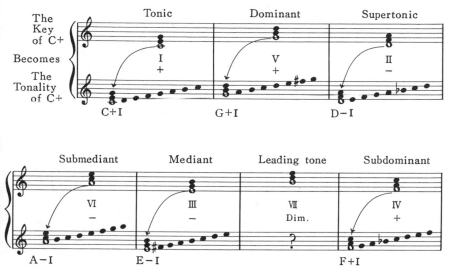

Note that the only triad in C major incapable of providing a key in the tonality of C is VII, whose diminished quality renders it unfit for service as a tonic chord. Only after its quality has been chromatically altered to minor (B−), or major (B+), can it be treated as a tonic chord.

The most closely related keys in the tonality of C minor are, similarly, those that grow out of the chords of the key of C minor. Like VII of C major, II, diminished in quality, is the one triad of the minor tonality which, in its original form, cannot become the tonic of a key. The dominant key exists in two modes: minor, springing from the pure minor dominant chord, and major, derived from the mixed minor dominant chord, as in Example 402.

Ex. 402

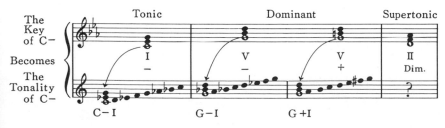

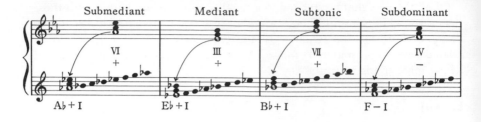

To summarize: keys in a tonality are related in exactly the same way that chords are related in a key. The construction of a key upon each degree of a tonality offers a convincing way of expanding or prolonging the chord that represents that degree. Finally, the keys that are most closely related in major tonalities are the dominant (+), supertonic (−), submediant (−), mediant (−), and subdominant (+); those most closely related in minor tonalities are the dominant (minor and major), submediant (+), mediant (+), subdominant (−), and seventh step (+).

THE PROCESS OF MODULATION

Key definition

The execution of a modulation involves two concepts which may be treated separately for convenience of discussion. The first has to do with the way in which a key may be established. This demands more than a mere employment of the tones that appear in its scale: it demands a definitive harmonic progression that clearly points out the whereabouts of the tonic. A simple way to accomplish this is the key-defining succession I-IV (or II)-V-I. For example, the chord progression I-V may be prolonged into a succession of keys by applying to each of the chords the key-defining progression of the key it represents as a tonic chord.

Ex. 403

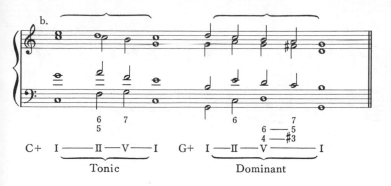

Pivots

1. *Tonic of the new key.* The second concept involved in the execution of a modulation has to do with the ambiguous relationship at the point where the change is made from one key to another. The harmonic analysis of Example 403*b* does not do full justice to the way in which we hear the modulation. The first I chord of G major is not apparent as such until the subsequent key-defining motion in the bass reveals the role played by the chord. As the chord is struck, our ears, under the influence of the fully established preceding key, interpret it as the V of C major. This chord has, in fact, two meanings: one in terms of the way in which it is approached, as V of C, and the other in terms of the way in which it is quitted, as I of G (Example 404).

Ex. 404

This ambiguous central detail of a modulation is called a pivot in view of the fact that the key change revolves about it. In Example 405 the equivocal function of the G chord in the second bar is clearly revealed by the approach to it as V of C. The subsequent definition of the dominant key establishes its new meaning as I of G major.

Ex. 405²

Tonic C+ I ——————— II—V—I ——— V——
          Dominant G+ I ——————— II—V—— I

The following examples, illustrating various modulations, employ uniformly a complete key-defining succession and consequently a pivotal chord which is the tonic of the new key. Observe first, the contour of the bass as it defines each key; second, the sequential nature of each example; third, the use of the tones of each key, particularly the use of the leading tone in the definition of minor keys.

Ex. 406

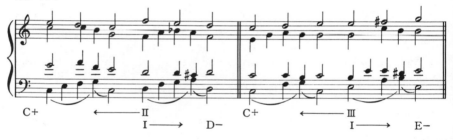

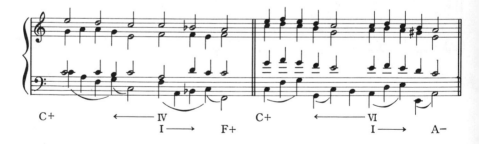

² Bach, Chorale, "In allen meinen Thaten," bars 1–4.

2. *Other pivots.* The transition from one key to another may be pivoted on a chord other than the tonic of the new key. For example, in tonic-dominant modulations I of the tonic key, which is also IV of the dominant, may be used as the pivotal chord by leading it directly to V of the new key. This results in a shortening of the key-defining succession, as the first tonic of the dominant key is not present. Of I-IV-V-I in G major, only the last three members, IV-V-I, remain.

Ex. 407

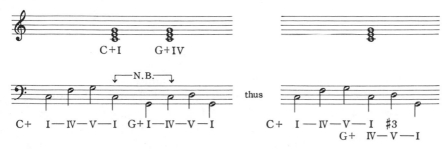

Example 408*a* illustrates a modulation with two complete key-defining successions; in Example *b*, I of C becomes IV of G with the consequent abbreviation of the definition of G. In example *c*, VI of C replaces the expected I and acts as II of G.

Ex. 408

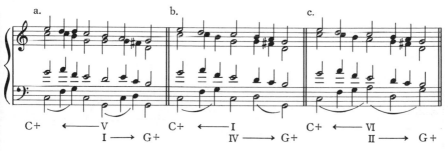

Examples 409 to 414 illustrate the use of pivotal chords other than the tonic of the new key.

Ex. 409³

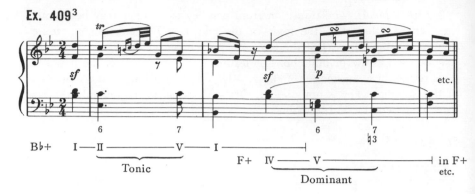

The first E chord in Example 410a reveals by its context that it is conceived horizontally as an application of the formula 8–5–8.⁴ It does not carry weight as a pivotal chord in the modulation to E minor; the first chord that reveals any E minor tendency is the following A chord which, characteristic of a subdominant chord, moves to V of E. The same remarks apply to the Brahms waltz of which Example 410a is a general sketch. The D-sharp

Ex. 410⁵

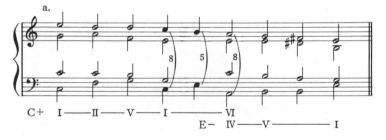

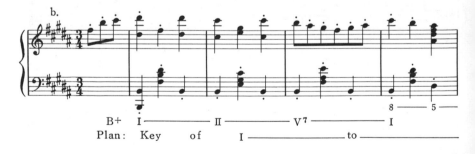

³ Beethoven, Sonata, Op. 22, last movement, bars 18–22.
⁴ Review Ex. 136a.
⁵ Ex. 410b, Brahms, Walzer, Op. 39, No. 1, Easy edition, bars 1–8.

chord in bar 4 has no harmonic meaning, but stands as a detail of voice leading between the B and G-sharp chords. The B in the bass of the first four
bars is an organ point.

Ex. 411[6]

3. Multiple pivots. Occasionally a progression, rather than a single chord,
plays a pivotal role in the execution of a modulation. In the following examples the influence of C-sharp minor carries through the F-sharp minor
chord. At the same time the tendency to move to E major commences with
the C-sharp minor chord (bar 2 of Example 411*b*).

---

[6] Ex. 411*b*, Beethoven, Sonata quasi una fantasia, Op. 27, No. 2, 1st
movement, bars 6–9.

The same remarks apply to Example 412.

Ex. 412[7]

4. Additional illustrations. There are two modulations in Example 413; the first from the tonic key A major to B minor, with V of A used pivotally as IV (with the third raised, hence mixed) of B minor, and the second from B minor to D major with I of B acting as VI of D major.

[7] Ex. 412*b,* Haydn, Sonata, Op. 42, last movement, bars 1–8.

Ex. 413[8]

Tonic A+

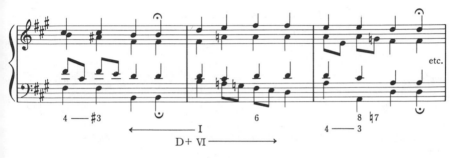

etc.

Modulations in the minor mode from the tonic to the pure minor dominant are the rule in fugal expositions. Example 414 is interesting for a number of reasons. It illustrates such a modulation with I of E-flat minor acting as the pivotal chord. Study the arresting rhythmic construction of the theme consisting of six beats plus four beats, a combination that conflicts with the steady march of metric pulsation. The bar lines in Example 414*a* and *b* have been drawn to indicate the rhythmic manipulation of the meter. The first two examples are cast in E minor to bring the modulation into more familiar ground.

[8] Bach, Chorale, "Werde munther," bars 3–8.

Ex. 414[9]

Applied dominant chords in modulation

The use of applied dominant relationships greatly enriches the means of modulation. The difference between an applied dominant and a modulation is the difference between detail and general plan. Applied dominant chords take their place as minutiae in the broader relationships that establish a key. For example, a bass and chord succession such as the following has only one meaning—it establishes, by its characteristic bass motion, the key of C minor.

Ex. 415

---

[9] Bach, *Well tempered Clavier,* Bk. I, Fuga VIII, bars 1–6.

Applied dominant chords will not interfere with the establishment of this key so long as the essential orientating relationships remain. These set the outlines of motion which can very easily accommodate applied dominant chords.[10] Compare the general plan of Example 415 with its execution in 416.

Ex. 416

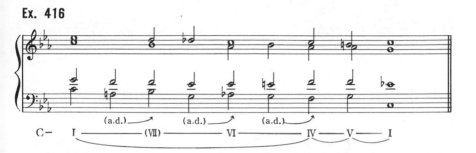

Similarly, a plan that involves modulation will readily absorb applied dominant relationships. An extension of Example 416 to include a modulation to the dominant raises as its initial tasks the establishment of first the tonic key, which we have already accomplished, and then the dominant key.

Ex. 417

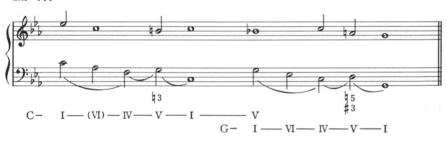

With the course of movement thus plotted, the rest is a question of particulars. Example 418*a* is a simple diatonic realization of the modulation; Example *b* uses applied dominant chords.

---

[10] Review the conduct of basses in the examples of Ch. 17 as a means of clarifying further the distinction between a modulatory action and the non-modulatory meaning of applied dominant relationships.

Ex. 418

The transition from key to key may be made through an applied dominant either to the tonic of the new key (Example 419*a*) or to whichever chord plays a pivotal role (Example *b*).

Ex. 419

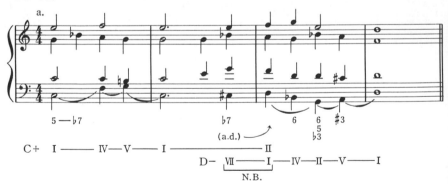

Example 420 illustrates a modulation from the tonic to the mediant key. The pivotal IV of F-sharp minor (also the II of A major) is stated first in its diatonic form, and immediately afterwards as an applied dominant. The voice leading with its 5–6–5 technique at the turn of bar 1, its suspension in the soprano of bar 2, and the leading of the bass should be studied.

Ex. 420¹¹

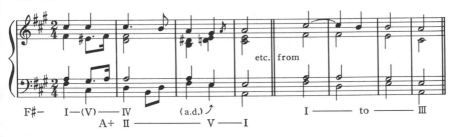

Example 422, illustrating the use of applied dominant color in a modulation from the tonic to the mediant is interesting in that I of the tonic key, G minor, is altered to assume dominant color to IV which becomes the II of B-flat major. The extension of the G chord in bars 4 to 6 with its passing tones should be approached through the sketches of Example 421.

¹¹ Schumann, 'Bunte Blätter," Op. 99, No. 4, bars 5–8.

Ex. 421

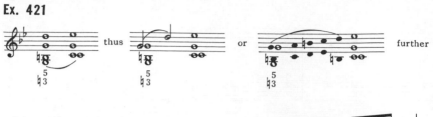

Ex. 422 [12]

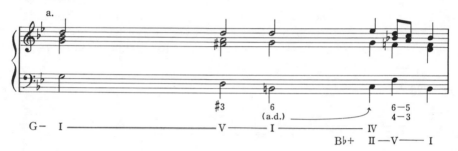

[12] Ex. 422c, Beethoven, Bagatelle, Op. 126, No. 2, bars 9–16.

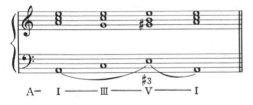

Modulation and Form

Minor mode

The technique of modulation has a profound influence on musical form. The establishment of keys carries with it a natural emphasis which delineates the broader rhythm of musical plan. A key succession which sets the framework of many compositions in minor is the movement from the tonic through the mediant to the dominant and back to the tonic.

Ex. 423

III in such a connection arises as a convenient bass tone through which to break in the more inclusive connection that reaches from I to V. In the following examples[13] each of these points is established as a key in a three-part form. The first part is concerned with the establishment of A minor and a modulation to the mediant with IV of A used pivotally as II of C, as indicated in Example 424.

[13] See Beethoven, Sonata, Op. 2, No. 2, last movement, bars 57–79, of which these examples are a reduction.

Ex. 424

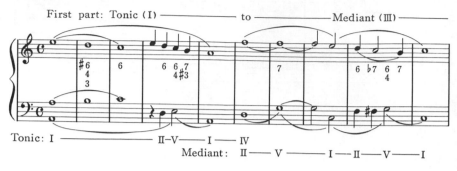

The second part (Example 425) fills in the third in the bass from the C chord to the E chord, which is subsequently defined as a key. Note that E minor, the pure minor dominant key, is established and at the last moment the third of the E chord is raised to increase its activity as V in the direction of I of A minor. The final part of the form is made up of a partial restatement of the first section and completes the broad outlines of the I-III-V-I plan by centering its activity in the tonic key.

Ex. 425

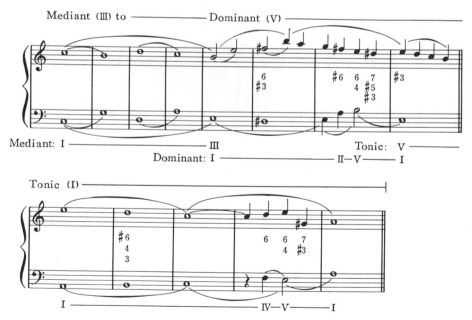

Major mode

A frequent major mode form grows out of the key succession tonic-dominant-tonic. In the examples[14] below, the succession grows into a three-part form in a characteristic manner, with the first part establishing the tonic and dominant keys, D major and A major. This sets as the essential task of the second part the reinterpretation of I of A major as V of D major, the tonic key, which is accomplished, by seeking out the tone G as the chord seventh. The final part reasserts the tonic key. In its simplest structural outlines the plan is:

Ex. 426

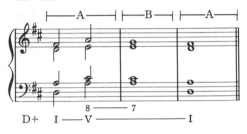

The first part of the form establishes the tonic and dominant keys by means of simple defining successions, making two phrases which are immediately repeated. In Example 427 the outline of the bass alone is given.

Ex. 427

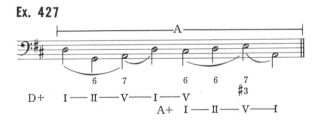

The more detailed second part, to be heard correctly, must be approached from its voice-leading origin. This is sketched in Example 428. Example *a* illustrates the simple stepwise motion that leads to the chord seventh, G, from the root, A. The expansion of this direct connection consists in the chord seventh's being fetched by the middle voice, C-sharp (Example *b*).

---

[14] See Beethoven, Sonata, Op. 28, Scherzo, of which examples 426–430 are a reduction.

Compare the stationary bass of Examples *a* and *b* with the passing bass of Example *c*, which, accompanying the upper voice, wins a G chord for this part of the form.[15] In Example *d* the bass, to gain space, doubles back upon itself and moves from F-sharp in sixths with the upper voice. For the rest (Example *e*) this simple technique is expanded to include fifths between the sixths. Thus the succession 6–6–6–6 becomes 6–5–6–5–6–5–6. The chromaticism results from the use of applied dominant color.

Ex. 428

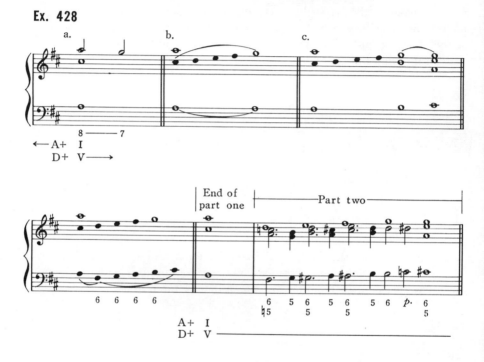

The thematic relationship that the second part bears to the first and third parts of the form is twofold: first, the octave skip that characterizes the upper voice of parts one and three is used in the bass of part two; second, a relationship not so obvious but active as a unifying force, the upper voice of the second part with its ascending motion acts as a foil to the downward break of the other parts.

Ex. 429

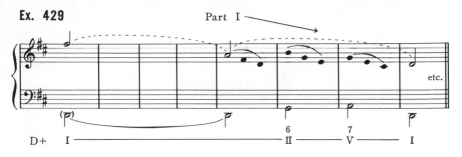

The third part recapitulates the material of the first part and completes the broad outlines of the form by reasserting the tonic key.

Ex. 430

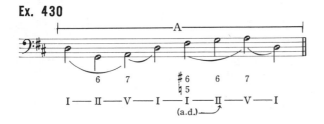

These two characteristic harmonic plans, one for the minor and the other for the major mode, with their illustrations, will indicate in a general way the constructive role played by modulation and voice leading in the delineation of musical design.

SUMMARY

The study of modulation embraces:
A. Key relationships. Keys are to tonality as chords are to key (Examples 401–403).
B. The process of modulation.
   1. The use of successive, complete, key-defining relationships. Pivotal chord is always the tonic of the new key (Examples 403–406).
   2. The use of abbreviated key definition. Pivotal chord is other than the tonic of the new key (Examples 407–414).
   3. Multiple pivots (Examples 411–412).
   4. Enrichment of modulatory techniques through the use of applied dominant color (Examples 415–422).
C. Modulation and form.
   1. A recurrent minor mode key succession, I-III-V-I (Examples 423–425).
   2. A recurrent major mode key succession, I-V-I (Examples 426–430).

Exercises

CHAPTER 2

Scales

1. Construct major scales from E, B, G–flat, F–sharp, and B–flat.
2. Construct pure minor scales from D, F, C–sharp, and E–flat in both the bass and treble clefs.
3. Construct all possible mixed scales, major and minor, from B, B–flat, G and D.

Melodic analysis

1. *Detailed analysis.* Of the following melodies, *a* and *c* are from Book II of the *Well tempered Clavier;* the others are folk tunes. In all cases the principal tones conform with the patterns of Examples 4 and 9. Use the melodic formations of Examples 6 and 7 as guides in analyzing the details of melodic construction. Note that dependent tones are easiest to recognize when they fall on unaccented parts of the bar. However, they often appear on accents, as in Exercise *d,* in which cases they displace principal tones without changing their meaning.

c.

d.

2. *Broad and detailed analysis.* Analyze the following folk tunes in terms of the procedures of Examples 18–22. First make a detailed analysis; then, employing the principal tones of the detailed analyses, make a broad analysis in which the structural relationship of each to the other is shown. Instructive analyses can also be made of the following fugue subjects from Book II of the *Well tempered Clavier:* F–sharp minor, G minor, A–flat major, and B–flat major.

a.

b.

c.

Fine

D.C. al Fine
Senza rep.

d.

CHAPTER 3

1. *Tempo*

An instructive way to learn about the interrelationship of tempo, meter, and rhythm is to play various recorded movements of quartets and symphonies by Haydn, Mozart, and Beethoven without consulting the scores until the following questions are answered:

a. What is the tempo? The answer may be given in terms of slow, medium, fast, or by use of Italian tempo terms.

b. What is the prevailing note value? What is the fastest, the slowest, note value?

c. What is the meter?

The answers, sometimes quite surprising, will be found in the scores. Other works and composers may be used for the same purposes, although baroque and twentieth-century pieces may cause difficulties.

2. *Phrase analysis*

Indicate the length of each phrase and hemiphrase in the following folk tunes.

3. Rhythmic groups

Indicate with a slur the length of each rhythmic group in the following folk tunes.

4. Melodic measurement

a. Regular meters. Indicate the meter and the position of the bar line of each of the following folk and folk-like tunes. Follow the recommendations of Example 36 and the sections, *Meter and rhythm* and *Melodic measurement.* In Exercise *b,* two different placements of the bar line should be tried. Play each version with exaggerated emphasis.

b. *Irregular and changing meters.* The following folk and folk-like melodies
are more challenging. In certain cases one irregular meter will scan the
entire exercise. In other cases one regular meter will do the same, but certain of the rhythmic groups will then cut across the bar line. Indicate all
such cross rhythms with a slur, or change the meter to accommodate the
uncooperative rhythm.

3.

CHAPTER 4

Measurement-absolute

1. Identify the following intervals in terms of numerical size and quality:

a.

b.

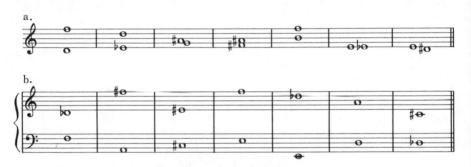

2*a*. Using A–flat as the lower tone, construct the following intervals: major second, diminished fifth, augmented fourth, minor sixth.

b. Construct from A the intervals listed in Exercise 2*a*.

c. Identify the inversions of the intervals constructed in Exercise 2*b*.

Measurement-relative

1. In which pure major and pure minor keys do the following intervals appear? In working out this exercise make use of Examples 57 and 59. For example: To determine the pure major keys in which the interval, D–flat—F, appears, first ascertain the size and quality of the interval. It is a major third. Then consult Example 57, where it will be learned that a major third has three scalar positions, 1–3, 4–6, and 5–7. Hence, our interval, D–flat—F, as scale steps 1–3, appears in D–flat major; as scale steps 4–6, it appears in A–flat major; and as 5–7, G–flat major.

2a. In which pure major scales does the minor sixth G—E–flat lie? Proceed as in Exercise 1.

b. By means of appropriate key defining successions, lead this interval to each of the major keys of 2a, above. Use Examples 64a and b as models.

c. Do the same with the minor third A-C.

Consonance and dissonance

1. Of the following intervals, which are consonant and which are dissonant?

2. Resolve each of the following dissonances to the nearest consonance in the major key indicated by the key signature. Consult Example 75.

3. In the following melodic fragments, principal tones have been provided with consonant support. Prepare at least two versions of each by providing consonant support for dependent tones (marked *) in the manner of Examples 76–79. Select accompanying intervals from the following: perfect octaves and fifths, major and minor thirds and sixths. Remember that the purpose of this exercise is purely exploratory; the results will probably be less than sensational. Try to make the lower voice as melodically purposeful as the upper voice.

f.

CHAPTER 5

1. *The Chord of Nature*. Construct the Chord of Nature, as illustrated in Example 82, from E–flat, F–sharp, A, D–flat.

2. *Chord qualities*. Construct a major, minor, and diminished triad from each of the following tones: E, G, A–flat, G–sharp.

3. *Chord names*. Construct a minor triad from F. In which major keys does it appear? What is its name in each of these keys? Repeat the exercise with major triads built from D, B–flat, and B; also with diminished triads from C, C–sharp, and D–sharp.

4. *Chord tones and positions*.

a. Identify the following triads in E–flat major. State the position and quality.

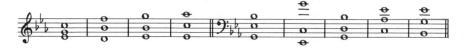

Example:

b. Construct the following inversions in the keys of A major and E–flat major: V_3^6, IV_4^6, I_4^6, II_3^6.

c. Construct the following positions in D major from the tones F–sharp, G, and A: $\frac{6}{3}$, $\frac{5}{3}$, $\frac{6}{4}$.

CHAPTER 6

1. Construct for four voices: G major, I_3^6, VI_3^5, IV_4^6; F major, II_3^6 III_3^5, I_4^6; D major, IV_3^5, I_4^5, VII_3^6. State the quality of each triad.

2. Construct for four voices at least six arrangements of V_3^5 of A-flat

major, V⁶₃ of A-flat major, and V⁶₄ of A-flat major. Exhaust all possible root doublings before resorting to other doublings.

3. State the name, position, and quality of each of the following chords. Which tones are doubled?

4. Assuming that each of the following chords has been constructed to represent the best possible vocal sonority, what criticism can be made with respect to voice range and the three rules of chord construction?

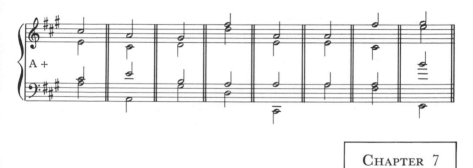

CHAPTER 7

In all of the following exercises use root position only.

1. Criticize and correct the chord construction and voice leading in the following successions. Do not alter the bass.

2. Prepare three settings of each of the following successions. In the first setting place the root of the initial chord in the soprano; in the second, place the third of the initial chord in the soprano; in the third, the fifth of the initial chord.

B major: I-V-I; I-IV-I; I-IV-V-I; I-VI-IV-V-I.

3. Notate in the bass clef the tones named below, so that they form a singable bass part. Regard them as so many roots; construct and connect the chords proper to each in conformity with the procedures described in Ch. 7.

In F major: F,C,D,A,B–flat,C,F; F,A,B–flat,G,C,F; F,A,D,C,F.

In G major: G,E,B,C,G,C,A,D,G; G,C,D,A,B,C,E,D,G.

In A–flat major: A–flat,D–flat,B–flat,C,A–flat,B–flat,E–flat,A–flat; A–flat,C,F,B–flat,E–flat,A–flat.

CHAPTER 8

Use root position only in all exercises.

Root progression by fifths

1. Construct the descending natural succession in E major and A–flat major. Prepare three settings of each, using a different initial soprano tone in each setting.

2. Move from I to III by means of the ascending natural succession and back to I by means of the descending natural succession. Place the succession in E–flat major and prepare three versions, making use of a different initial soprano tone in each version.

3. Construct the compact descending succession (I-IV-V-I) in F major and A major. Prepare three versions of each.

Other root progressions

Insert tones in the bass at the points marked with asterisks. These inserted bass tones may be employed as elements of the natural succession, associate chords, or chords that lie a second a part. They may also be considered a means of correcting faulty voice leading, harmonizing dependent tones, or filling in an interval in the bass. Sometimes they will play more than one role. Indicate the role or roles played by each inserted tone. Fill in the alto and tenor. Slurs throughout this exercise point out figures and sequences as discussed in the section, *Figure and Sequence,* Ch. 9.

a.

b.

c.

d.

e.

f.

g.

h.

i.

CHAPTER 9

Use root position only.

Choral style, four parts

1. *Figured basses.* Complete the soprano and fill in the middle voices.

2. *Drills.* Write a cadencing soprano over each of the following basses. Fill in the alto and tenor parts.

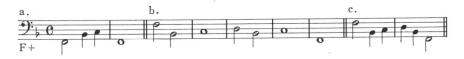

3. *Harmonization of melodies.* Follow the suggestions of the section, *The procedure,* in harmonizing the following folk and folk-like melodies. Observe the character of each melody. The main burden of harmonization should

be given to I, IV, and V chords. Reserve associate and other chords for dependent tasks.

Keyboard style, three and four parts

1. *Figured basses.* Use keyboard style and notation. Exercise *a.* is to be set for four parts; *b.* for four parts and then for three; *c.* for three parts.

c.

2. *Drills*. Set complete cadential basses and chords to each of the following fragments. Start in each case with I.

3. *Harmonization of melodies*. Harmonize the following folk and folk-like melodies in four part keyboard style and notation.

CHAPTER 10

1. *Drills*

a. Set voices in four part choral style above the following bass to form $\frac{5}{3}$ or 6 positions. Construct the soprano for the entire drill before placing the inner voices.

F+

b. Many techniques can be fashioned out of the $\frac{6}{3}$ and its alternation with the $\frac{5}{3}$. Several are suggested below. Treat each one sequentially, and continue with it until an ending presents itself. In some cases it will be necessary to modify the concluding chords in order to add conviction to the close, but in most cases the sequence will end conveniently on the octave above or below the starting point. If necessary, lead the voices beyond their normal limits. Make note of the weak points (usually involving the diminished triad) in each setting. It will prove difficult (in some settings) but instructive to add a fourth voice to each completed three part setting. Parallel motion will prevail in most of the settings.

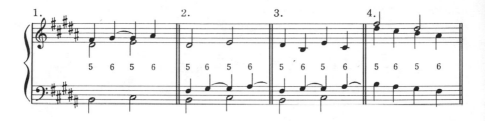

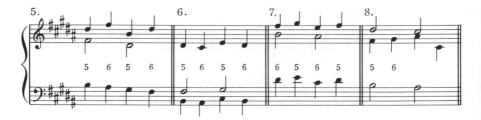

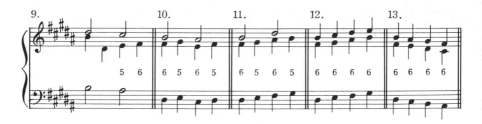

2. *Figured basses*

Set for four voices, choral style.

a.

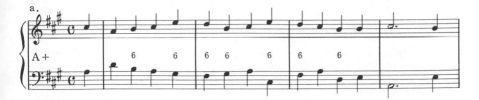

Du Friedefürst. Chorale (adapted)

b.

Uns ist ein Kindlein. Chorale (adapted)

c.

Aus meines Herzens Grunde. Chorale (adapted)

3. *Figured basses, incomplete*

Insert chords in either the $\frac{5}{3}$ or 6 position at points marked with an asterisk.

a.

b. In keyboard style, four parts.

cadential bass

c.

d.

4. Unfigured basses

The positions of chords are not specified. Set each exercise for four voices, employing $\frac{5}{3}$ and $\frac{6}{3}$ positions. Examine each narrow context and fix the identity of principal chords before turning to details. Note in *b* and *c* that the soprano and bass of the first phrase become bass and soprano of the second, thus creating simple examples of a device known as invertible or double counterpoint.

a.

b.

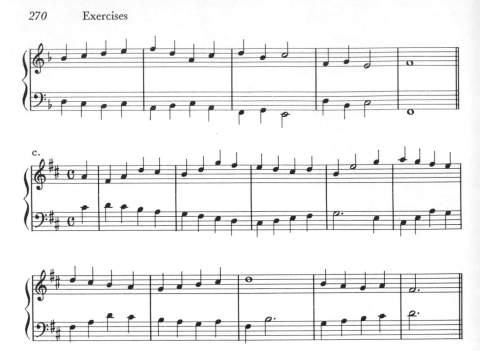

5. *Harmonizations*

Set melodies *a* and *b* for four voices, choral style. Exercise *c* is to be set for four parts, keyboard style.

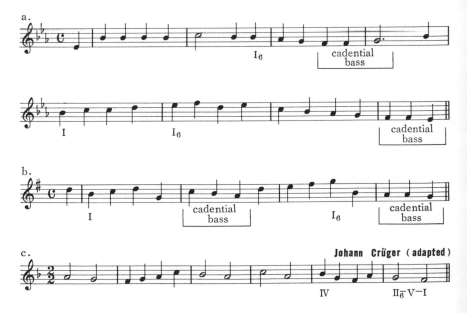

CHAPTER 11

1. *Drills*

a. Set Drill *a* of Chapter X in F minor. Pay attention to the treatment of the sixth and seventh steps in the bass of bar three.

b. Construct the following successions in E minor and C–sharp minor: I-IV-V-I; I-VI-V-I; I-II^6-V-I; I-IV^6-V-I. Take care to avoid the melodic progression of an augmented second. Construct the bass before setting the upper voices.

c. Fill in the inner voices in keyboard style, four parts. Study each progression in which the seventh step appears before deciding whether it should be treated as a leading tone or left in its original form.

2. *Figured basses*

Mark off the cadences. For the meaning of accidentals in figured bass, review the section, *Chromatic Figured Bass Signatures.* A dash between numerals indicates that the tones represented by the numerals must appear successively in the same voice.

a.

b.

c.

d. Leggiero

e.   Andante con moto. In keyboard style, four parts.

Fine

dal segno al fine

3. Figured basses, incomplete

Insert bass notes at asterisked points to represent $\frac{5}{3}$ or $\frac{6}{3}$ positions.

4. *Unfigured basses*

a. Set *a*, *b*, and *c* for four voices, choral style.

b. Accidentals have been withheld throughout. Examine all progressions in which the sixth and seventh steps appear (in inner as well as outer voices), before deciding whether they should be raised chromatically or left in their original form.

c. Follow the directions for 4*b.*

d. For three voices, as indicated in bar 1. Do not add or alter accidentals.

5. *Harmonizations*

CHAPTER 12

1. *Drills*

　　a. Construct in G minor and G major one example of each characteristic use of the $\frac{6}{4}$.

　　b. Set the following cadential basses three times in F minor. Use a different soprano tone in the opening chord of each version.

c. Examine the metric organization of each of the following cadential melodies. Set a bass and inner voices to each one in four part keyboard style, employing, wherever possible, one form or other of the $^6_4$, stable and unstable. Start in each case with I in $^5_3$ position. Describe the function of each $^6_4$.

d. Follow the directions stated in Drill *c* in setting the following cadential melodies. Use four part choral style.

2. *Analysis*

The following unusual instances should be analyzed with reference to the harmonic meaning of each six-four position.

a. Beginning and end, 2nd movt., Seventh Symphony, opus 92, Beethoven.

b. Opening bars of the song, "Die Mainacht," opus 43, no. 2, Brahms. The text should be translated, for Brahms is employing a symbolism in his six-fours in these and parallel bars. It is instructive, in this instance, to compare Brahms's melody and bass with those of bars 7–12 in the F–sharp major Impromptu, opus 36, Chopin.

c. Bars 15–17, Prelude, opus 28, No. 14, Chopin.

d. Bars 7–10, 3rd movt., Sonata, opus 110, Beethoven. See also the parallel passage in the 4th movt. at *L'istesso tempo di Arioso.*

3. *Figured basses*

Describe the use of each $^6_4$.

a.
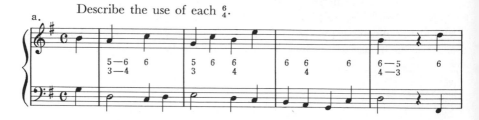

b.

c. In keyboard style, as indicated in bars 1–2.

4. *Unfigured basses*

Mark off the cadences and fill in the inner parts, employing all positions.

a.

b.

5. *Unfigured basses, incomplete*

Employ $\frac{5}{3}$, 6, or $\frac{6}{4}$ positions at the points marked with asterisks, inserting bass tones where they are needed.

a. In four part keyboard style.

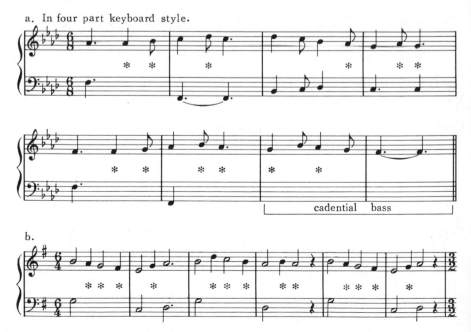

John Dowland (adapted)

6. *Harmonizations*

Mark off the cadences. Construct the bass before filling in the inner voices.

a.

b.

c.

d. Siciliano. In keyboard style, four parts.

CHAPTER 13

1. *Drills*

    a. The descending succession provides a good testing ground for the use of tones of figuration. In the drill that follows, the succession appears four times in various positions, with a cadence added at the end. Suggestions for the use of figuration tones are subjoined; they need not be followed.

b. The same bass may be used in C major. It will prove more hazardous because of the impoverished nature of VII. Less simultaneous eighth note motion and a three part setting will lead to greater success. Do not follow the suggestions subjoined to Drill *a.*

c. The following figured basses have been abstracted from three settings of the Chorale, "Helft mir" by Bach. Fill in the middle parts and insert tones of figuration in a rhythm, not necessarily continuous, of eighth notes. Compare your completed settings with those of Bach who makes interesting use of accented tones of figuration. The most striking of the settings is 3, of which bar 2 merits careful analysis.

d.[1] Analyze the following excerpts. Identify the underlying chords and the tones of figuration. What factors cause the parallel fifths in each example?

[1] Ex. 1, Sonata, Op. 101, last movement.
    Ex. 2, Prussian Sonata No. 1, last movement, Nagels Musik-Archiv, No. 6.
    Ex. 3, Cantata No. 59, Duetto.

1.

2.

3.

2. *Figured basses*

a. Complete the soprano and fill in the inner voices. Add passing tones, neighboring tones, and chordal leaps in a eighth-note rhythm to the bass up to each cadence.

1.

Chorale (adapted)

2. In keyboard style, four parts

b. Construct the inner voices. Add tones of figuration to the upper parts as the opportunity to do so presents itself. Do not use more than one tone of figuration at a time.

c. Construct the inner voices. Add tones of figuration to the outer voices. Wherever it is possible to do so, insert tones of figuration in the inner voices in such a manner that they move in parallel thirds and sixths with the outer voices.

d. Add tones of figuration to all parts but not to more than two parts simultaneously.

3. *Unfigured basses*

a. Fill in the middle voices in four part keyboard style to represent the various triad positions. Add tones of figuration throughout.

b. Tones of figuration are included in the following exercises. Very few, if any, should be added to the inner parts. Observe throughout the employment of accented neighbors and passing tones, and note how they disguise the essential outer voice relationships.

1.

3.

4. Harmonizations

The bass has been suggested, though not in its real register, at problematic points. Both folk tunes offer opportunities for an imitative use of eighth notes in the bass and inner parts.

a.   Sturdily

b.   Moderato

CHAPTER 14

1. Drills

a. Interpolate suspensions in the following three voice successions to win new intervals and break up parallel fifths.

A +

b. Complete the following by adding one middle part containing very few, if any, tones of figuration.

c. Analyze the voice leading and the use of tones of figuration.[1]

[1] Ex. 1. Chorale, "Schaut, ihr Sünder," beginning.
Ex. 2. Chorale, "Helft mir" (Cant. 183), bars 4–6.
Ex. 3. Chorale, "Freu' dich sehr" (Cant. 30), beginning.
Ex. 4. Chorale, "Herzlich thut" (Christmas Oratorio), beginning.
Ex. 5. Chorale, "Gelobet seist du" (Cant. 64), conclusion.
Ex. 6. Solemn Mass, D minor, Kyrie.
Ex. 7. Sonata, Op. 106, 1st movt.

1.   **Bach**

etc.

2.   **Bach**

etc.

3.   **Bach**

accompaniment

etc.

4.   **Bach**

etc.

5.   **Bach**

6.

Cherubini

7.

Beethoven

etc.

d. Harmonize each drill with a complete cadential bass starting with I. Introduce direct and indirect anticipations into the soprano in an eighth note rhythm.

1.   **2.**

3.

2. *Figured basses*

a. Complete the soprano and fill in the inner voices. Add suspensions throughout.

1. In four part keyboard style.

2.

3.

b. Introduce direct and indirect suspensions in an eighth note rhythm.

c. For three parts. Decorate the inserted part sparingly. Abbreviations are explained in Example 285.

3. *Chorale harmonizations*[2]

Complete the bass. Fill in the inner voices. Add tones of figuration in the style of bars one and two. The figured bass indications have been omitted from Exercise *b.*

[2] Ex. *a.* See Bach, "Herzlich lieb hab' ich dich."
Ex. *b.* See Bach, "Jesu, Jesu, du bist mein."

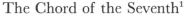

CHAPTER 15

The Chord of the Seventh[1]

1. Drills

a. Construct each of the following exercises three times. Use a different soprano in the opening chord of each version. Indicate with a slur the dissonant tones and their resolutions. Repeat each drill in D minor in four part keyboard style.

[1] The exercises appear under three headings: *The Chord of the Seventh, Expanded Treatment of the Seventh,* and *Pseudo Positions,* in agreement with general headings that appear in the text.

b. Harmonize the following sopranos with the chord succession, I to either IV⁷, or II$^6_5$ or II⁷ to V⁷ to I. Select the second chord in the succession by testing all three in each exercise. Indicate with a slur the dissonant tones and their resolutions.

c. Continue each of the following successions sequentially until a convenient opportunity to end with the tonic triad presents itself. Build each sequence on the descending natural succession. Construct each exercise in E major and in E minor.

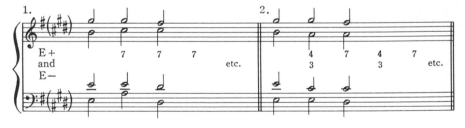

d. Continue the following exercise sequentially as in Drill *c* above. The exercise is to be constructed in both G major and G minor.

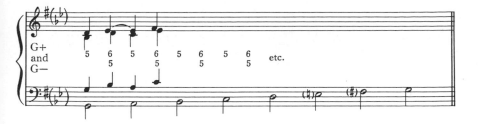

2. *Figured basses*

a. Describe the use of each chordal dissonant tone in terms of its melodic function as an expanded passing tone, neighbor, or suspension. Interpolate tones of figuration.

b. Describe the use of tones of figuration.

3. *Unfigured basses*

a. Fill in the inner voices to represent triads and seventh chords in various positions.

b. Follow the directions for *3a*. Try to maintain a half note rhythm in the inner parts in bars 5 and 6.

Expanded Treatment of the Seventh

1. *Drills*

a. Analyze the treatment of chordal dissonances.

b. Describe the treatment of all dissonances.

1.

2.

3. In four parts, keyboard style.

4.

2. *Figured basses*

a In four parts, keyboard style.

b. Bars 8 to 11 require complementary eighth notes in the inner parts. Count bars 8 and 9 as three groups of two beats each. Such a cross rhythm is known as a hemiola or sesquialtera.

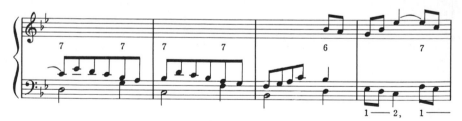

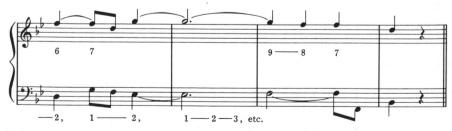

3. *Unfigured basses*

a. Employ triads and chords of the seventh in normal and manipulated fashion.

sesquialtera

b. Insert bass tones at the points marked with asterisks. Construct the inner voices. Make use of triads, seventh chords, and prolonged sevenths.

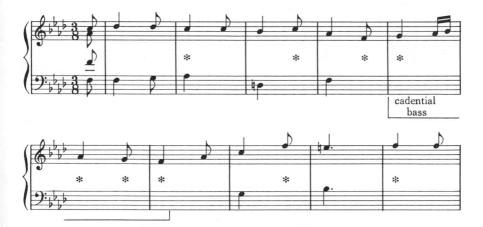

cadential
bass

4. *Harmonizations*

In setting the following melodies, four tone chords should be treated normally, except where context indicates that one or another of the manipulated uses is advisable. Proceed as usual from the general to the particular.

a. Harmonize the following melodies, which appear in exercises for preceding chapters: Chapter 2, *Melodic Analysis* 2e, Chapter 3, 1d, 2a.

b. **Moderato**

c. Use the suggested chords in the positions that make the smoothest connections. Employ a four part keyboard style.

Pseudo Positions

1. *Analysis*

Analyze the following excerpts for the use of four tone chords, real and pseudo.[2]

a.

Schumann

etc.

b.

Mozart

etc.

[2] Ex. *a,* Song, "Ich grolle nicht."
Ex. *b,* Quartet K 387, 3rd movement, Trio.
Ex. *c,* "Es ist ein Ros' entsprungen," Op. 122, No. 8.

c.

Brahms

2. Figured bass

Describe the treatment of seventh chords and the use of pseudo positions.

3. Unfigured basses

a. Make use of triads, chords of the seventh, and pseudo positions in filling in the inner voices. Employ a four part keyboard style.

b. Follow the directions for 3a, but use a four part choral notation.

CHAPTER 16

1. *Drills*

a. Construct the successions I-IV-V$^9_7$-I and I-V$^9_7$-I in A major and in A minor. Construct each succession twice: first with the ninth in the soprano and then with the ninth in an inner voice.

b. Construct the descending natural succession in F–sharp major and in F–sharp minor with ninths in alternate chords. Employ the pattern, 7-$^9_7$-7-$^9_7$, etc.

c. Analyze the following excerpts. Examine the context in which each ninth appears.[1]

[1] Ex. *1,* Bach, Cantata 150, Ciaccona.

Ex. *2,* Beethoven, Op. 81a. This echoic use of the postilion's call should be studied in conjunction with the entire first movement.

Ex. *3,* Brahms, Intermezzo, Op. 119, No. 1.

Adagio

3.

2. Figured basses

a.   In four parts, keyboard style.

b. Account for *four - three - two* in bars 1 and 2

c. Broadly

3. *Unfigured basses*

Make use of the suggested inner voices.

CHAPTER 17

1. *Drills*

a. Construct an applied dominant on each of the following tones. Be sure to cancel accidentals of the key signatures wherever necessary.

b. Construct the appropriate applied diminished seventh before each of the following chords.

c. Construct the following succession: I, to II$_5^6$ as an applied dominant, to V$^{8-7}$, to I, in D major, D minor, E major, and E minor.

d. Construct the succession, I, to IV^7 as an applied VII^7, to V^7 to I. Use the keys of B major, B minor, F major, and F minor. Employ a four part keyboard style.

e. Employ the following formula to construct applied dominants to triads in G major and G minor:

$$I—\text{applied dominant (V or VII) to} \left\{ \begin{array}{l} \text{II (in G major only)} \\ \text{III} \\ \text{IV} \\ \text{VI} \\ \text{VII (in G minor only)} \end{array} \right\} —\text{applied}$$

dominant (V or VII) to V$^{8-7}$ to I. Construct the outer voices first, then the inner voices.

f. The following drills are all related through the technique that is employed. Fill in with only one middle part. The third exercise is an abstract of the introduction to the first movement of Beethoven's First Symphony, which should be analyzed in conjunction with the drill. See also the opening bars of Beethoven's opus 28, and the C major Prelude, Book II of *The Well tempered Clavier.*

g. Apply the descending natural succession to the following sopranos in G major (drill *1*) and G minor (drill *2*). Construct each chord so that it assumes dominant color to the chord that follows. Do not alter the first and last chords in each drill. In setting the G minor soprano, study the distance between the roots of the succession VI⁷-II⁷.

2. *Figured basses*

a. Prepare two versions of the following drill. In the first version construct the drill diatonically. In the second version, chromatically alter each ⁶₅ and 7 (except the 7 in bar seven) so that it becomes an applied dominant (V or VII) to the following chord.

b. Chromatically alter each 7 so that it assumes the color of an applied diminished VII⁷ to the following chord.

c. Fill in the inner voices. Explain the use of chromatically altered tones. Which are the principal chords?

3. *Unfigured basses*

a. Chromatically alter chords to create applied dominant color. Do not insert any chords.

b. Compare with Schumann, *Nachtstücke*, opus 23, no. 2. Use a four part keyboard style.

c. Compare with Schumann, *Gesänge der Frühe*, opus 133, no. 5. Use the normal divided notation.

CHAPTER 18

1. *Drills*

a. Employ the following scheme to modulate from the tonic key of D minor to each of the closely related keys: (1) Establish the tonic key; (2) modulate to and establish the new key. Indicate the pivotal chord.

b. Harmonize the following modulating sopranos in four part keyboard style.

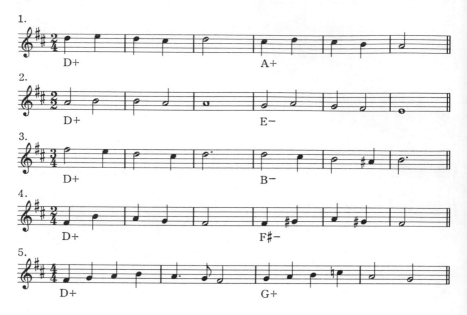

c. Construct the following figured basses for four voices. To what keys is modulation made? Locate the principal chords.

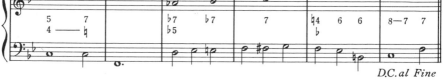

b.

2. *Figured basses*[1]

The melodic progression of an augmented second should be avoided in chorale style. Voices, especially inner voices, may cross occasionally and adjacent parts may, at times, exceed the spacing limit of an octave.

a. "Nicht so traurig, nicht so sehr."

[1] See *371 Harmonized Chorales and 69 Chorale Melodies by Johann Sebastian Bach,* ed. Albert Riemenschneider. New York: G. Schirmer, Inc., 1941. See also, J. S. Bach, *Lieder und Arien,* Lea Pocket Scores, No. 74.

b. "Jesu, meine Freude."

c. "Ermuntre dich, mein schwacher Geist."

d. "So giebst du nun."

3. *Unfigured basses*

a. "Valet will ich dir geben."

b. "O wie selig seid ihr doch."

c. "Ich freue mich in dir."

4. *Harmonizations*

Chorale melodies.

a.

"In dir ist Freude"

b.

"O Traurigkeit, O Herzeleid"

c.

"O Herzensangst."

Folk tunes and other melodies. Use a four part keyboard style.

a.

Schwesterlein

b.

So nimm denn meine Hände

c.

Csardas kis kalapot veszek

d.

from "The Beggar's Opera"

from "The Beggar's Opera"

5. *Analysis*

a. Analyze the Menuetto and Trio of Beethoven's Sonata. opus 2, No. 1. Relate the progression of keys to the tonalities of the pieces.

b. Study the C major Prelude of *The Well tempered Clavier*, Book I, in conjunction with the following unfigured bass.

c. Study the F major Prelude from Book I of *The Well tempered Clavier* in conjunction with the following figured bass.

d. Make similar reductions of the C minor, A minor, and B–flat major Preludes, Book I.

e. Analyze the second movement, Allegro molto, of the Sonata, opus 110, by Beethoven. Rhythmic features deserve careful study.

f. Analyze Menuetto I from the Mozart Sonata, K 282.

g. Analyze the theme (Tema) and selected variations from the Mozart Sonata K 284.

Index

Index